O Chaplain! My Chaplain! Man of Service

Conversation, Prayer and Meditation
with
The Last Living D-Day Chaplain of Omaha Beach

Love love love . . .

Janelle Frese

Janelle T. Frese
with
Colonel Chaplain George Russell Barber,
USAFR

Note for Librarians: a cataloguing record for this book that includes Dewey Decimal Classification and US Library of Congress numbers is available from the Library and Archives of Canada. The complete cataloguing record can be obtained from their online database at:
www.collectionscanada.ca/amicus/index-e.html
ISBN 1-4120-4354-9
Printed in Victoria, BC, Canada

TRAFFORD

Offices in Canada, USA, Ireland, UK and Spain
This book was published on-demand in cooperation with Trafford Publishing. On-demand publishing is a unique process and service of making a book available for retail sale to the public taking advantage of on-demand manufacturing and Internet marketing. On-demand publishing includes promotions, retail sales, manufacturing, order fulfilment, accounting and collecting royalties on behalf of the author.
Book sales for North America and international:
Trafford Publishing, 6E–2333 Government St.,
Victoria, BC v8t 4p4 CANADA
phone 250 383 6864 (toll-free 1 888 232 4444)
fax 250 383 6804; email to orders@trafford.com
Book sales in Europe:
Trafford Publishing (uk) Ltd., Enterprise House, Wistaston Road Business Centre, Wistaston Road, Crewe, Cheshire cw2 7rp UNITED KINGDOM
phone 01270 251 396 (local rate 0845 230 9601)
facsimile 01270 254 983; orders.uk@trafford.com
Order online at:
www.trafford.com/robots/04-2162.html

10 9 8 7 6 5 4 3

To my army of spirit allies and their commanding officers,
Harry Lindgren
Murray Hamilton
Nathan Cohen — long live Books on Main Street

JTF

For my dear family, with undying love,

For preachers and teachers who know God above;

To Chaplains everywhere, now and then,

Who've brought to God, good women and men;

For all our Veterans far and near,

And those who died, we hold you dear.

CONTENTS

A SERVICE BULLETIN

```
    G
G   O   D
    O
    D
```

INVOCATION

Dear Reader,

I would like to begin with a prayer. Please pray with me. My prayer for you as you read this work about my life story is that you will feel the peace and the presence and the power of God in your life at this time and forever more.

I pray that every need that you have in your life will be fulfilled by the power of God and of Christ and of His Holy Spirit. May you each one walk with Him in love and obedience and service to others all over the world.

Amen
Colonel Chaplain George Russell Barber, USAFR

JT's TESTIMONY

God must have said, "*It is time,*" when He put me in a room with my dying grandfather. Before, I'd been walking my own way through life, stumbling into meanings that never occurred to me. Being the eyewitness in my grandfather's death gave me God's purpose for life. I would later understand it as the prerequisite for the huge undertaking of writing this book about Chaplain Barber, the man who would save me from sorrow and change my life forever.

Chaplain Barber is one of the few men on Earth who has had to witness and deal with death and human suffering every day. In God's way, this book about the Chaplain's life is my recovery from the pain of loss, a personal gain in the mainstream of my life.

I bear witness to you today that every life experience prepares you for the next, and when you least expect it you can count on God to make your day, *His way*. I'm grateful for this lesson. It teaches life on purpose for a good cause.

JTF

SERMON

THE MEETING OF THE EYES

It was September 11th, the annual antithesis of my March 11th birth date. The year was 1999, the end of a millenium. A new beginning. I was on edge sitting at my grandfather's bedside, cradling him in my arms as he called out to his mother who wasn't there. I whispered back to him through quiet tears, "You're the bravest man in the world."

"Mom," was the last thing he sighed before his eyes opened wide to tell me more.

Grandpa had the bluest twinkle-light Santa eyes that lit up my childhood every time I searched them. As he lay dying in my arms I longed to keep that connection. I looked for myself in his eyes, but became lost in a hue of blinding blue.

Some say the eyes are the *windows to the soul*. It's just possible they tell its story as the reflection of *you* making your appearance in another's eyes. In the meeting of our eyes my grandpa and I knew this kind of story. Love. Family. This served us well. It was home.

When the old *Me* vanished in his eyes that night, a new light energy of bright golden Godbeams waved wonder back at me. Inside Grandpa's windows to his brave soul, white–gowned angel arms welcomed like soft glistening dove's wings opening the gates to *Grandpa's Heaven*.

In this glorious open space, I saw his spirit grow too big for his body to contain. In his eyes where I looked for answers all my life, I found magnificent mystery. In my eyes, the drowning pools of my first live death, I held onto my history hoping to hear him say in a simple way this was okay.

"Everything good comes from God," he always said, *"with an extra 'O' in it."* In his transition, more than *okay*, there was love, the greatest gift of service one can give another. Love. O positive exchange!

In letting him go I found him again, standing tall next to me, proud of the woman I was becoming. I dared not say *goodbye*, just *away*, for this was my ready-room preparation for understanding my mission in the *MEETING OF THE EYES*.

* * *

It was on a cool morning in May when I first met Colonel Chaplain George Russell Barber, Ret. USAF. I was among hundreds who had gathered for the 2001 Memorial Day services being held in the tiny thriving city of La Palma, California, my hometown. Chaplain Barber was one of several featured speakers, but the only one who spoke to me, the only one I heard.

Earlier that morning I had accepted a coffee-talk invitation from my father to walk to the Civic Center for the celebration. I kept time with Dad's patriotic pace and arrived just in time for the invocation. Bowing my head I stared at the ground and let my eyes wander around to meet Dad's shoes. My Dad, the former Mayor, was teeter-tottering in his shoes on the City Hall lawn.

I jabbed him gently in the ribs. He put his hunky arm around me and I drifted into long ago kid thoughts of all the shoe polishing I did for him more than once upon a time. I never finished a pair of shoes until I could see my reflection in them.

Dad's shoes. My reflection. Myself in Grandpa's eyes. Military Man's voice filled my head heavy. In the prayer I reflected.

All the influential men in my life slide-showed before me on my mind's eye movie screen. Grandpa Ted, Uncle Irv, Harry and Jack. My dad, my brother, always watching my back. Teachers and preachers fond and dear, all my guides young and old, far and near. All people everywhere doing the best they can. Men and women making sacrifices in service to others, for God, for Country, for other men's countries, for family, home. *Amen*.

I looked up through red, white and blue balloons, binocular style, all the way to the microphone. There I witnessed Chaplain Barber, risen to the podium from his front row seat. He mixed the invocation with spicy oration, Southern style, which permitted *Amen, D-Day, horses* and *ice cream* to flow in the same sentence.

He shared holy rolling stories about a good life of service, participation in three wars...making the landing on Omaha Beach...comforting dying soldiers...helping to rescue Korean orphans. I watched and listened intrigued.

I wasn't alone. Little American flags flapped in the air above dozens of citizens sitting jaw-awed as the Chaplain told his eight-plus decades worth of stories about service to fellow man, friend or unfortunate foe.

Politicians, police and fire officials, mourning the loss of a fallen comrade, nodded loud and clear. Way in the back of the black folding chair section, some folks slanted and craned their necks looking to get closer to the public showing of glowing war veteran.

Through his recollections, Chaplain Barber took me to distant lands and back to my memories of Grandpa. I closed my eyes open to see him with me again.

Drifting back in time I heard Grandpa whistle, "*Wooh!*" whilst I sat on his lap for *The Bear Story*. Then he warned me, "*The goblins 'll git you, ef you don't watch out,"* and my eyes bugged out. It was *Little Orphant Annie* come to our house to stay. I heard them all in a hurry, Grandpa's favorite poems by his mother's favorite poet, James Whitcomb Riley.

For morning snack attacks Grandpa flipped flapjacks onto my highchair tray. We sipped Swedish coffee in wee tea cups, and I heard the whispering words I'll always remember him for. They filled the crisp, Southern California spring air on this day to remember, *"Everything good comes from God, with an extra 'O' in it."*

Back in my body, I heard Chaplain Barber finish with those same words made simple, like a Church hymn, *"Praise God that good is everywhere."* He raised both hands in the air offering the victory signs. Double peace to me. *"Peace,"* hit me hard for *good*, if I'd been wearing any socks surely they'd have been knocked off. I covered my mouth to conceal the mystery unfolding. I looked up and found myself standing alone in rays of Godlight. *If through our battles in life we can learn to see the good things, there may be peace.*

This was Chaplain Barber's message unraveling. He closed with the three talking 'P's of prayer – *peace, presence* and *power*— of God. Taking in the talk I studied his walk. His was a slow, flat, but sure-footed shuffle. Like Grandpa! He lured me to the eternal flame.

Maneuvering my way through moms and dads chasing tots chasing balloons, I made my careful approach along the path to the Memorial wreath. "Chaplain Barber," I said, "I enjoyed your speech today so much," and reached for his hand to shake.

He appeared comfortable and confident in his well worn Air Force blues. His thin white hair was cut short, clean and combed back slick. I followed the rim of his glasses past his hairline down the ranks to his full bird shoulders. *Colonel* Chaplain George R.

Barber. I never knew chaplains soared so high. His decorations dizzied psychedelic as I followed the seams of his pressed uniform to his shiny black patent-leather shoes. They reminded me of all the quarters I'd earned as a kid. *His need polishing*, I thought, as I gazed back up in search of his eyes.

With my athlete's posture and his well-suited stance we stood dead even at about six feet. About me someone said, "There's a tall drink-o'-water." I rolled my eyes to shrug off the embarrassment and waited while the Chaplain combed through the contents of his grey briefcase for several seconds.

I added, "Your story is so inspiring. It would make a great read. Where can I find your book?" He fingered through fading white Xeroxed copies of newspaper articles, crumpled tissues, and Gideons pocket Bibles.

"I haven't written one," he finally responded. Eyes buried deep in his briefcase he handed me one paper after another, all local stories on him. I accepted them graciously and said, "You know, your story would make a great read. You ought to put it all down in a book."

He slowly glanced over at me for the first time. In the meeting of our eyes the message became crystal clear, the extra *Oh!* of why we are here.

"Oh?" he said.

I saw straight through his glasses and right into his eyes. They were bright blue twinkling like Santa eyes. I saw my reflection in them. Instantly, I was smiling the *Me* I was meant to be.

Looking for himself in my eyes, he reached for my hand, took it and said, "How about you and I get together and talk about that?"

So we did.

And so it is.

I

D-DAY

*"I prayed like it was only up to God, and
I dug like it was only up to me, and together
we dug that hole pretty deep."*

—Chaplain Barber, June 6, 2001

ᏛᎱᏛᎱᏛᎱᏛᎱᏛᎱᏛᎱ ✦ ᎠᏫᎠᏫᎠᏫᎠᏫᎠᏫᎠᏫ

I made the decision to call Chaplain Barber after more than a week of torturous self-deliberating doubt. I was so afraid of risking who I was for who I could become, I locked myself out of all possibility. The only way out of this personal paralysis and into *what could be* was prayer.

I surrendered to God and I prayed like it was only up to Him. Then I picked up the phone and dialed like it was only up to me.

It was June 6th, 2001. In the digital din of our phones connecting, I thought I heard a faint echo of my grandpa's voice, *"Everything good…"* I felt Grandpa standing behind me, his true gentleman's hands upon my shoulders once more. God's way of calling.

"Chaplain Barber, this is Janelle Frese. We met on Memorial Day."

"I know who you are," he said and gleefully added, "you're Ji-neel come to write my book." His pronunciation of my name put a smile on my face. I liked his genteel Georgia spin on it.

He quizzed me, "You know what today is?"

"It's D-Day," I answered.

"That's right. Fifty-seven years ago, one thousand, five hundred and thirty-one of my men died on Omaha Beach. I remember it like it was yesterday."

"Have you thought any more about telling your story?" I brought him up to date.

"Well, I tell my story wherever I go, but I think it's probably time it gets published."

Chaplain Barber selected *Jack's Salad Bowl* on Whittier Boulevard for our fellowship hall. I arrived disheveled from the drive, but discarded all negative thought, took a deep cleansing breath and headed for the front door. I walked past a variety of vending machines into the foyer, turned right, looked up, and there I saw the Chaplain. He was dressed in his beloved uniform, overstuffed grey briefcase by his side. He sat content in the large corner booth, his reflection bouncing off the front window. He was waiting for me.

Past the lollipop counter I paced, made a right-face, then stepped up to greet him at what still remains our sacred site. There in the bountiful booth we shared our first of many meals. From lemonade to last supper we took turns talking, swapping stories, sipping coffee, enjoying chats with God and Jesus and friends who just happened to be there.

When my little girls would join us, Chaplain Barber guided them in prayer. He called on Jesus to bless us and keep us. I called him, "Chaplain." He called me, "Ji-neel." He put us all together on a first-name basis with the Lord.

After three years of conversation, prayer and meditation came the meaning of our meeting—our friendship forged of service, his message, a timeless legacy.

On June 25th, 2001, we enjoyed the grand opening main course, a discourse, prelude into prayer. We broke bread and I asked the leading question, "Chaplain Barber, if you could tell the world your story, where would it begin?"

"Probably D-Day," he said.

"Why?" I asked.

"So much happened that day."

THE FIRST TAPE...

CHAPLAIN: We sailed across the channel on larger ships and when we got to within about four miles of the beach I called the ship to prayer, everybody on the ship, some of them took off their helmets even. We prayed that we would have God with us during this great event so we could bring freedom to the world.

JANELLE: Can you describe what you looked like?

CHAPLAIN: I was six feet tall, blue eyes, dark almost black hair, and shaved to the scalp that day. It was easier to keep your head clean that way. I could take my bath in my helmet.

JANELLE: What did you carry with you?

CHAPLAIN: I carried a backpack with my Bible and things I needed to use. Not much. I had already given out lots of pocket- sized Bibles to the men.

JANELLE: You had no weapon?

CHAPLAIN: Chaplains carry no weapons, so I only had the *Armor of God*. The men had their backpacks on with all their equipment. I first saw death by seeing bodies in the Channel. I asked, "Are we going to pick up those bodies?" The other officers said, "They'll get picked up later on."

Our job was to get over the side of the ship and into smaller landing ships and get on shore. In the Higgins boat there were thirty-one men and gear. I was the only officer with thirty enlisted men, privates to sergeants. We went over the side of the larger ship down rope ladders to get into the Higgins boat.

JANELLE: What did you do once you were in the landing craft?

CHAPLAIN: We talked as we went in and we prayed. I told them I believed God would prevail. We talked about doing this for our loved ones back home. We prayed for our country and we prayed for this day to be a success. When we began to weave our way into the shore there were bodies floating in the water, even that far out, men who had started the landing earlier in the day. When we got closer to the shore there were lots of Higgins boats around us. One about forty meters from us had hit a mine and blew up, killed everybody. The bodies were floating in the water with the pocket Bibles bobbing.

JANELLE: What time was your boat making its way in?

CHAPLAIN: Well, (we) had started landing at about 6:30 in the morning. I landed with my men at about 2:00 in the afternoon. I led my men off. I walked out through the shallow water. Gunfire was all around us. Men were crying and praying and helping each other. I went to the men who were wounded. We were all trying to help each other out. Our men were shooting at the Germans and throwing hand grenades. Some of my men were getting killed. The Germans were firing at them all up and down the beach. Men were wounded, some of them were dying. I got to as many of them as I could, talked to them, shared with them.

JANELLE: What did you say?

CHAPLAIN: I said, "Now, I'm your Chaplain and I'm here to help you. God is going to see us through. God knows you. He loves you. If you have to make the supreme sacrifice God will help you. He's prepared a place for you in His kingdom." I prayed like everything was up to God you see. Wounded men were crying for help. We had medics who landed with us too to help. They tried to bind up the wounds along with the chaplains. Other chaplains made the landing, but only four chaplains landed on Omaha Beach on D-Day.

JANELLE: And you are the last?

CHAPLAIN: I think I am, sadly.

JANELLE: How did you survive D-Day?

CHAPLAIN: There was a big cliff about a hundred feet high that our men were trying to get over. Germans were shooting down at us. I couldn't get off the beach or get over that cliff either. When night came, and at that time of year in June it didn't get dark until 11:00 at night, I began to dig my own foxhole. I realized I wasn't going to get off the beach so I began to dig.

I dug as if everything depended on me and I prayed as if everything depended on God and together we dug that whole pretty deep into the cliff there. I could get my head under there and keep clear of the bullets. Every other bullet was a tracer bullet, lighting up that sky that whole night from 11:00 to 3:00.

JANELLE: Was there any air support?

CHAPLAIN: We couldn't send the planes in because they'd hit our own men and everything flying would be shot at. Germans were flying that night. Our paratroopers had started their drops beginning at midnight. A lot of them died too you see.

JANELLE: Describe the moment you were first able to climb out of your foxhole. What did you have to do?

CHAPLAIN: I started climbing out of the foxhole at about 2:30 in the morning. It was still dark then. Our men had been able to destroy enough of the enemy to be able to get over that cliff by about 3:30. They were also able to get around the cliff and build little paths. We were still being shot at, of course. German officers were screaming at their men to take us out. But our enemy had finally been hit pretty good by then and we had cleared a way to get up the hill. My friend was one of those heroes. He landed before I did. He is a medal of honor winner, Walter Ehlers of Buena Park. He was wounded and his brother was killed on Omaha Beach that day.

JANELLE: Did you ever get hit?

CHAPLAIN: No, I never did.

JANELLE: How does that make you feel?

CHAPLAIN: I'm grateful. You know, I just prayed that God would spare me and spare my men too. There's no rhyme or reason or sense to war.

JANELLE: You've said you had the *Armor of God* protecting you. What does that mean?

CHAPLAIN: Just my faith.

JANELLE: Is faith what saved you?

CHAPLAIN: Maybe so. I don't know why I wasn't hit, but I wasn't. We used five beaches to land, but no beach was as dangerous as our beach. The Germans were most prepared on Omaha beach. One thousand, five hundred and thirty-one of *my men* died on Omaha Beach that day. I don't know how many were wounded. The good news is within twenty-four hours we put fifty thousand men across the beaches. We lost 400,000 Americans in World War II. War is hell, but this had to be done.

JANELLE: You were the youngest chaplain at age 30. How old were most of the men who died there on the beach?

CHAPLAIN: They mainly ranged in ages from 17 to 20. Just young men you see.

JANELLE: How do you compare with other survivors of D-Day in terms of being able to talk about it?

CHAPLAIN: I can talk about it. Not many survivors can, but I've had to talk about it and listen to it, as a chaplain and a minister, I had to. It was difficult, but I saw it as my duty I was honored to perform.

JANELLE: I have a dark picture in my mind of men and the things they carried strewn across the sands of Omaha Beach. It makes me curious to know, of the things you carried, what survived the beach?

CHAPLAIN: I had most of my things packed in my Jeep on a different boat which had sunk. The driver of my Jeep floated up and swam to shore. They didn't pull my Jeep out of the water until about a week later. By the time we worked our way inward from there, I only had my Bible with me in my backpack. The only thing I ever had that survived the war is my Bible.

JANELLE: That's a message.

CHAPLAIN: That's a message isn't it?

JANELLE: Like an anthem. With respect to D-Day, besides carrying the message, what other duties were you responsible for carrying out?

CHAPLAIN: Well, we had to bury the dead. I walked with a team of people to help select the site. We had body bags because there wasn't time or caskets for all of the men. We had to dig the grave and say a prayer.

JANELLE: What words could possibly justify all that?

CHAPLAIN: "God bless you and save you and keep you forever in His love and His power and give you eternal life in the place He has prepared for you." It was a short prayer because there were hundreds of them. Dog tags told their faith.

JANELLE: Was that *fate* or *faith*? What do you mean?

CHAPLAIN: The dog tags indicated what faith, what religion, each of the men believed in or subscribed to. I was the Protestant chaplain. Once in a while there wouldn't be a Catholic chaplain to pray over a Catholic soldier so I'd say the prayer. It didn't matter. They all deserved God's love and comfort. Just as long as we pointed their souls to God, "*God has accepted you into His kingdom and you will live forever. No more war, no more suffering, no more death, and you will join your loved ones.*"

JANELLE: How was the news delivered to their loved ones?

CHAPLAIN: The War Department took care of sending word home. It varied how long it took, but as soon as they could. Some of the people wanted their sons and husbands shipped home and we would do that if we could. Often times we had to bury them and then dig them up. We knew where they were and we kept the dog tags. We tried to do everything we could to let those families know that there was someone there that cared.

JANELLE: Did you bury any of the enemy?

CHAPLAIN: Yes. We buried some German soldiers. Not in our cemetery, but in another location. Once a person's dead, they're no longer the enemy. I gave them the same Christian burial I'd give to anybody.

JANELLE: You've referred to the multitudes of soldiers as, "*your men,*" like you knew them all.

CHAPLAIN: That's right. In those sermons on the Sunday before D-Day I spoke to all of them. So they were all my men. You see I love everybody. Sometimes I don't like certain things, but I love everybody. I have to.

JANELLE: And that makes developing relationships part of your work.

CHAPLAIN: Exactly.

JANELLE: You've seen a lot of death and presided over hundreds of funerals.

CHAPLAIN: Thousands.

JANELLE: At the site in Normandy, did you have to bury anyone that you were, perhaps, especially close with?

CHAPLAIN: I never had to bury them, but two of my assistants died later in the war. One of my drivers and my organist. Terrible shame. You know the acts of courage I witnessed that day on June the 6th, young men giving themselves in service to their country, for freedom, trying to defeat an enemy many of them couldn't even see, it's hard to describe, but I think you get the picture.

Chaplain Barber's D-Day became my vision after our first interview. I know it may not have happened exactly like this on June 6, 1944, but on the eve of June 25, 2001, one of Chaplain Barber's men revealed his living D-Day experience to me in my dream.

"Chaplain?"

"Yes, Brother?"

"Do you have a favorite verse from the scriptures?" The Private First Class from Cincinnati tried to keep calm aboard the Higgins boat to the beach.

"Right, Brother, well, I like John 3:16, *For God so loved the world, that He gave His only begotten Son, that whosoever believeth in Him should not perish, but have everlasting life.*"

"Mm-hmm," the soldier nodded, "everlasting life? Do you believe that's all I have to do, Chaplain? Just believe I'll have an everlasting life?"

The Chaplain smiled at his soldier, "Did you pray with me on Sunday?"

"Yes, sir, I did."

"Do you remember what we prayed about?"

"...*to have faith and understand that God loves us.* Right?"

"Go on," urged the Chaplain.

The young soldier rolled his eyes over to his buddy who shouted out, "SO WE CAN SAVE THE FREE WORLD FROM EVIL MEN LIKE HITLER AND MUSSOLINI!"

"Right, yeah, right. That's what I said," the Chaplain paused, "He loves you, Brother. God loves all of you, and through the sacrifice of His Son, our Savior Jesus Christ, there is a place prepared for each one of us. You hold onto that faith now, okay?"

"Yes I will, Chaplain," The Private from Cincinnati promised.

"Me too," said his buddy.

"Right, okay. That's good. Did y'all get a Bible?" The Chaplain surveyed all thirty of his men with a single tilt of his head and reached into his backpack.

"I have mine right here in my pocket, next to Shirley." The Private quivered a smile as he felt for his girl first.

"Right, that's good." Chaplain Barber instantly knew in his heart that his wife, Helen, was praying for him that very moment. The moment was strong, but fleeting, like his delicate Southern self-assuredness.

"That's good," he said.

That's good ricocheted in the last remains of the Chaplain's good hearing. The explosion knocked soldiers into each other as the transport forty meters in front was mine-ripped apart, scattering men and arms and pocket Bibles high into the foaming tides.

The Chaplain held onto a shaken soldier as a father would his frightened boy. Struggling to regain equilibrium, glazed eyes scanning the scene, the Chaplain remained calm in the front of the boat where everything happened at once.

He couldn't hear himself speaking the words, "*...Even though I walk through the valley of the shadow of death, I will fear no evil...*"

He couldn't feel the tears rolling down his sweatsoaked cheeks. He couldn't taste the salt or the blood or the oil in his mouth. He could only see the tiny floating funerals. Writhing Bibles. Bobbing grave-markers in a sea of red madness.

In a flash of heat and ocean spray, the Chaplain found himself leading his men out of their Higgins boat and on through the thrashing water tumbling onto shore.

God's Armor, a glowing white body shield deflecting all bullets and bombs, maneuvered the Chaplain like a ghost across the beach. And like the Holy Ghost, he was there inside the wounded man, comforting the dying man, everywhere at the same time, pealing back to reveal truth and freedom through eyes of blue hope.

The soldier from my dream died on the beach that day, his pocket Bible lay beside Shirley on the sand. In the dream he invited me into his open eyes. He wanted me to see what he experienced that long day in the eyes of his Chaplain.

When I gazed into the dead soldier's eyes the reflection I found was not my own, but something I'd seen only once before. In his eyes, the drowning pools of his first live death, there was beauty, glorious golden white light shining. Sunlight flashes on gliding white dove's wings. Angel's wings, white doors opening the gates to *Private Heaven*. Shirley. His mom. Open arms. Going home.

II

FELLOWSHIP

A Monument for the Soldiers!
And what will ye build it of?
Can ye build it of marble, or brass, or Bronze,
Outlasting the Soldier's love?

—James Whitcomb Riley

ᏩᎵ ᏩᎵ ᏩᎵ ᏩᎵ ᏩᎵ ᏩᎵ ✝ ᎠᏁ ᎠᏁ ᎠᏁ ᎠᏁ ᎠᏁ ᎠᏁ

On the Sunday before D-Day, Chaplain Barber delivered God's message to military personnel of all ranks and sizes on eleven different ships in Weymouth Harbor, England. At the ripe old age of 30, he may have been the youngest Chaplain in all the branches of military service.

JANELLE: Tell me what you said to the troops on June the 4th, 1944.

CHAPLAIN: On the Sunday before D-Day, the Catholic Chaplain and I took some lunch. We were in Weymouth Harbor in England. We held services on eleven different ships there. He would hold a Catholic service and I would hold a Protestant service. From morning until dark, we went from ship to ship in a little motor boat and gave sermons and gave out thousands of Bibles. We had hundreds of thousands of men training in England, and we had equipment, any kind you could think of.

June the 5th was when we got on the ships to take us across the channel toward France and the beaches, about thirty or thirty-five miles. Of course, we had men and equipment on those ships too. They fed us pretty good too. We didn't eat Spam on the 5th!

Anyway, on Sunday I gave out a lot of Bibles because there are no atheists in foxholes. Those men were anxious to get a Bible. I said, "Remember your mother, your father, your brothers, your sisters. They all love you. They are praying for you too," and I quoted the 23rd Psalm, and emphasized God is in control.

"We're on His side and we're going to win." That was the matter-of-fact way I talked to them all of the time. "Jesus gave his life for us and we may have to give our lives for Him and for our country. He knows all about it and He's with us here." Just before I went over the side to go on the LSVP I stood on the bridge of the ship and used the P.A. system and had a prayer for everybody on the ship. General Eisenhower prayed too with his Chaplain just before he gave the word to go. I quoted John 3:16.

JANELLE: *For God so loved the world that He gave…*

CHAPLAIN: His one and only Son. Right. And I shared with them, telling them that God understands all this and He will see us through. I tried to inspire them, "We've got to do this and liberate the world from the Nazis and socialism and communism and atheism and all these evil institutions.

JANELLE: Do you remember any of the men in those services?

CHAPLAIN: Oh, sure I do. Many of them. In one of those services was Ernie Pyle, the war correspondent. He said, "Chaplain, I will see you on the beach!" Now, he didn't get ashore until the next day, D plus 1, in the morning, but when he came we sat down and had a can a Spam together. I don't know when, but sometime after, he went out to write his story.

JANELLE: Do you think there is any synchronicity in your meeting Ernie Pyle?

CHAPLAIN: Why, yes. I do. When Ernie Pyle walked the beach he set out to write a story. As he walked he saw all the death and destruction and carnage. When he came along the body of a soldier who had died there on the beach, he reached down and picked up the little pocket Bible that soldier had carried. It had that soldier's name in it. Ernie Pyle carried it for a while, then he laid it back down on the beach. Now I can't prove it, but it's just possible that I gave <u>that</u> soldier <u>that</u> Bible on <u>that</u> Sunday before D-Day.

JANELLE: What does that mean to you?

CHAPLAIN: It means a great deal. Many people in the world remember Ernie Pyle and the importance of his writing. It's a shame he was killed later in the Pacific. To know that Ernie Pyle and I made a connection says a lot to me.

When I was in New Orleans for the dedication of the D-Day Museum (last year) I spoke five times. There were many people there, including celebrity guests and noted others. I gave the opening prayer, and later that day Tom Hanks got up to speak. He read the dispatch about Ernie Pyle's experience on the beach. That's all he said. It was the most sacred five minutes of the whole five days I was down there. It was one of the greatest speeches I've heard.

The audience was spell-bound. We all know what a great actor Tom Hanks is, and I thank him for bringing that message to the world. And I'm glad I had a part in the distribution of those Bibles that Sunday before D-Day. When I sat and listened to Tom Hanks, I remembered that can of Spam and thought about how it was possible that the Bible in that story was one I gave out to one of my men.

You see the experience of giving out those thousands and thousands of Bibles gave a lot of men hope. If that soldier trusted in what that Bible stood for then he could feel protected. He could be saved. Now I'm not going to get into who gets saved and all like that because God's going to choose who's saved and who's not, but I believe that Bible contains the truth that leads to freedom, for everybody.

Ernie Pyle's story and the fact he was in one of my services fits into my whole life as a chaplain and a minister and a speaker. Just today, I gave out a dozen pocket Bibles to the people who brought me to their meeting, *Marching Through History*, and I told this story. People connect to it and they feel its power.

JANELLE: There's power in possibility.

CHAPLAIN: Yes there is and the Bible makes it possible for people to have hope.

JANELLE: And to have hope is one step closer to freedom.

CHAPLAIN: That's right.

JANELLE: That's powerful.

CHAPLAIN: Absolutely.

JANELLE: When we've prayed together, Chaplain, you've asked God to allow us to feel His *peace, presence* and *power,* three 'P's for a better world. Do you think all chaplains try to evoke that kind of energy?

CHAPLAIN: In many ways, part of a chaplain's duty is to keep things as positive as possible. All chaplains try to send God's message, no matter their denomination.

JANELLE: How strict in your religion did you have to be as a Chaplain?

CHAPLAIN: Well, I'm a Christian, a Protestant, and my faith is completely Christ-centered; but I had a lot of men who either had no faith to begin with, or they were Jewish or Catholic or some other denomination. It didn't matter to me. I loved them all you see.

JANELLE: What Jesus would do?

CHAPLAIN: I suppose that's right. When I sailed over on the *Queen Mary,* they called her the *Grey Ghost,* I held services for the Jewish men on Saturday and the Protestants and the Catholics had theirs on Sunday. Everybody deserves to be treated right and that's right by God. I don't get into theology with anybody. I like to keep it simple.

JANELLE: Were you treated right by everybody?

CHAPLAIN: Why, yes, I think I was. Everybody seemed to like me and I liked everybody too. And as a Chaplain I had the privilege of associating with the highest to the lowest in rank from generals to privates and all in between. See, the Chaplains don't have to go through protocol if they want to talk to the General or to the Colonel or to a private. You just go directly to him, you don't have to go through channels. I would confer with anybody and everybody and share and so on.

JANELLE: Did you ever confer with any British or European military or civilian allies?

CHAPLAIN: General Montgomery ate at our mess. Also, soon after we landed in France we picked up a young man from Belgium called Francois Vaxelier. I've got his name in my book here. So while we were in Liege where the Germans had pushed us back, he asked me, "Chaplain, can you take me back to my home up in Brussels?"

I said, "Sure, Francois." Now I didn't know him other than he was a nice young man about twenty years old and an interpreter for us. He spoke all the languages - French, German, English, of course - but I said, "Sure hop in my Jeep." So we drove up to the top of the hills in Brussels. We got up there and we walked into a mansion. His father was a Baron. His father owned the *Au Bon Marche* stores which are a chain of high level department stores all over Belgium.

They just welcomed me with opened arms because I brought their son home they hadn't seen in months and months. They introduced me to everybody and put me to sleep there. They let me sleep until 8:00 o'clock in the morning. The maid came in and she drew my bath.

I also met a man there who was visiting. He owned a chocolate factory. He furnished me with boxes and boxes of chocolates to take back to my soldiers. I took Francois home a few times while we were waiting there to continue our march through the war. After the war I kept in touch with him, the whole family. He had three brothers and one sister. There were five children. One of the brothers got killed in a ski accident years later.

I made several trips back to Europe. In the mid-Eighties I was in Europe visiting and I found myself in Brussels one day. I went into the *Au Bon Marche* store and I said, "Can you tell me how I can get in touch with Francois Vaxelier?"

"Oh, you mean the Baron," this nice lady store clerk said. His father had died and Francois had inherited the business. They said, "Wait!"

So I sat over in a nice comfortable chair for a little while and about twenty minutes later he called on the phone for me. He said, "Oh, Chaplain, I'm so glad to hear from you. I just came from America. I've got jet lag, but," he said, "please come over to my apartment tomorrow for lunch."

So I went to his apartment for lunch the next day. His apartment was right next door to the house I'd taken him home to and his mother still lived there. We talked and talked and talked over a wonderful lunch. He was a collector of art and traveled all over the world. In the home he had tapestries worth over $600,000 dollars.

He said to me, "When you were here, Chaplain, there were 1500 employees working the stores. Now there are 28,000! I'm buying whole companies. Find me a company in America I can buy!"

We figured up his net worth on the New York Stock Exchange at about $300 million dollars and that was in the mid-Eighties. Recently, I spoke to the *Battle of the Bulge* group at a big restaurant in Santa Fe Springs. The featured speaker that day was the Belgian Consul General from Los Angeles. I talked with him and shared the stories about Francois. He said that company now has 50,000 employees just here in America.

Francois has now gone onto Heaven. But I've kept in touch with his family. Just last month I talked to his widow.

JANELLE: What a treasure you found in Francois.

CHAPLAIN: I thank God for allowing me so many opportunities to share and make connections with so many people and so many things over these times of war and times of peace. I was there to help people. I brought as many as I could to a closer walk with Christ. I baptized some people. The Chaplaincy has allowed me to do a great and many things.

JANELLE: Even war allowed you time for fellowship. But I'm curious, how were you able to hop in a Jeep and drive to Brussels with Francois when the war was going on?

CHAPLAIN: It was during a time when we had pulled back from Germany into Liege. We had established our camps and everything around there. See, for R & R my situation was a little different because, being a chaplain, I was free to move around. I could take a day or five or whatever as needed. If I did use that freedom, I'd fill those days trying to find things I could take back to my men.

One night, a truck driver, one of ours, got lost with his truck full of gasoline, five gallon gasoline cans. He said, "If you help me unload this, I'll give it to you."

So we helped him. The next day I took some of those cans in my Jeep and took off for Paris. That was really the only recreation time I had during combat. My driver drove me to Paris. We stayed in a little place and took in all the sites. We visited Notre Dame. On the way there I met a friend about thirty miles out of Paris. She had a young son, about eleven. My driver told her it was my birthday and she baked me a cake. It was August the 26th, 1944. She also had a home in Paris and that's where we stayed. I tried to stay in touch through the years but I've lost track of her now.

JANELLE: Chaplain, can you take me back to the beach and build back up from there?

CHAPLAIN: Of course. Soon after the shelling on the beach and making it up the cliffs to bury the dead, I remember one night sleeping beside the hedgerows when German planes flew over and made a drop on us. Over 200 men got hit all around me. That was a terrible experience.

Later on, about a week after, I took a little spotter artillery plane and flew down the beach, saw Utah Beach, and on to Cherbourg which had just fallen. We flew low, just above the hedgerows, so the Germans couldn't get a bead on us. That was an interesting experience.

The Germans had us blocked off at St. Lo. We had to have our planes fly over and literally bomb a path, maybe a half a mile, through the German lines. We concentrated our tanks to go through there while marching our men through too, in an effort to swing in behind the Germans and surround them.

We took some German prisoners. We treated them very well. Many of them were destined to be sent to America. They laughed at us and said, "We are headed for America and you are headed for Germany!"

July the 20th is *St. Lo Breakthrough*. In that experience our spotter planes came over and fired smoke flares to show our bombers where to drop. Unfortunately, some of that smoke drifted back and some of our planes actually bombed some of our own men, killed by friendly fire.

JANELLE: That's terrible.

CHAPLAIN: Yes it is, but this was war and sometimes things like that happen.

JANELLE: But that mission was accomplished.

CHAPLAIN: Right. And I had to follow along on all kinds of maneuvers like that. My mind wasn't always on spiritual channels. I had to follow the tactics of war too. I looked at every aspect of what was happening. That way, too, I felt I was better prepared to serve my men.

JANELLE: What happened after the breakthrough?

CHAPLAIN: After the breakthrough, we were enabled to start the march across France and on into Paris. We got near Paris and held up so General De Gaulle could come in and lead the march to liberate Paris. Some of our units swung north through Southern Belgium on toward Germany. I was among the group that went north. So I didn't get to see Paris until later.

JANELLE: On your birthday.

CHAPLAIN: Yes! That's one of the reasons I went back that way on R&R. I guess I remember R&R so well because it is a happy memory.

You know, all across Europe we were constantly in danger, but we kept on pushing the Germans ahead of us all the time.

I also was at a little place in France, a crossroads with a cafe there. Three days before I got there, a hundred of our men had given up to the Germans and they were disarmed. The SS came along with their tanks and just mowed our men down. I was there just three days after that happened.

On one of my trips back to Europe I visited the lady who owned the cafe there. We talked and talked about that experience. It brought back a lot of memories, some sad and some good. She was thrilled to have me visit her.

An interesting aside, the Germans had some horse-drawn artillery units, and some cavalry units too. We had bombed those and their horses were killed. After we liberated Paris I saw those roads littered with horses and dead Germans. That just struck me hard that day.

We went on through Liege and after establishing our camps we got acquainted with our Belgian friends there. That's when Francois told me he hadn't seen his family in nearly a year. That's why I took him home.

JANELLE: Everybody needs a little R&R. Even the Chaplain.

CHAPLAIN: Even the interpreter. Boy, I couldn't do his job. I'd be so tongue-tied. You see, everybody had a different duty to fulfill, a special role to play that was meant especially for them.

JANELLE: How long was your tour of duty in the European theatre?

CHAPLAIN: I spent eleven months and three days in the firestorm across Europe. We marched across France, fighting and praying all the way. Our division moved across France and into Germany. (We) had built two main highways from the beach to Germany. One headed one way from the beach to Germany, called *Red Ball Highway*, and the other went back to the beach.

After we got into Germany and took that first German city, which was Aachen, the Germans pushed us out. Our supplies couldn't keep up with us. We were still hauling our supplies to our troops there from the beaches you see. So the Germans came in with more supplies and more people to kick us out of Aachen and push us back to Liege. We didn't retake Aachen until after the Battle of the Bulge.

I lost hundreds of my men there too. The Germans broke through our lines and I had a Jeep hit by a German artillery shell. One of my assistants was killed. That was terrible. That was where the German general wanted our general to surrender to them, but our general said, "Nuts to you!"

JANELLE: How many Jeeps did you have?

CHAPLAIN: Well, I had one Jeep that sunk in about fifteen feet of water on D-Day. But they resupplied me, you see. After D-Day I got a new Jeep, a trailer and pump organ. When this one got wrecked, they supplied me with another one. They always kept me supplied with everything I needed. They tried to do that for everybody, making sure we had access and availability to whatever we needed. Of course, in the heat of battle, that wasn't always the case.

One Saturday afternoon we were preparing to go across the Rhine over the Remaugen Bridge. I had it in my mind to hold services on the other side on Sunday. So I was preparing for those services. When we got about a mile or so from the bridge I saw it go down. The Germans collapsed that bridge. We had to get there fast to help rescue men who had been there ahead of us. Two of my men died in my arms. Supposedly, for that reason, my name went around the world via media wire.

JANELLE: How did you hear your name was in the news?

CHAPLAIN: I was told, and later in a letter from Helen, my wife, I learned there was some confusion about it at home because in civilian life I'm called Russ Barber, but in military life it's George Barber. But I was there. Fortunately, our engineers had built two pontoons, so we were able to get across. We held those services the next day.

JANELLE: Your tour took you to some of the most dangerous places during the war. Have you visited any of those war memorials since your retirement?

CHAPLAIN: First, let me say that a chaplain really never retires from service. I'm always there to pray and to share, so I'm still serving. I'll always be of service.

But I ended the war with Patton. A great memorial to Patton was built out in Indio. That's where he trained his troops. There was a great celebration out there the day we dedicated it to him. I was there. Kitty Bradley spoke too. I remember her telling me she remembered about the ice cream and she told me to tell about the ice cream!

JANELLE: Tell me about the ice cream.

CHAPLAIN: Okay. Well, in England they were trying to conserve all the milk for the babies. So you couldn't get ice cream and we all missed it.

I went down to a Rotary meeting one day in Bournemouth. I said, "Do you know anybody that has old fashioned ice cream freezers so we could make some ice cream?"

The man there across from me said he had two Swedish ice cream freezers sitting up in his attic. He offered to sell them to me. I bought them up and brought them to our mess sergeant. I said, "Let's make some ice cream."

He said, "Sure!"

I was with the special headquarters troops who set up the mess in the First Infantry Division. We probably had 20,000 men in the First Division.

Now every mess is only as good as its mess sergeant, you know. So all through my career there could be good meals or bad meals, depending upon where I was. A mess sergeant would get an allocation of money to buy local food. Most of it would be delivered. In Europe we made good use of local food. The food was pretty dull in England, but once we got to France, we picked up some French cooks who did wonders with the GI food. That was nice.

Well, when the Generals were planning our invasion they used to come down from London quite often and eat at our mess. We had the *best mess*. On the trial run of the ice cream there was enough for the whole group to eat. We made vanilla and chocolate. Generals Eisenhower, Bradley and Montgomery loved it so much they each had two servings. That's how ours always remained known as the "best mess!"

Word spread about it too. The French people heard about it and they'd have ice cream cones for us when we came by. I'd give out candy bars. Now, whenever I mention the ice cream, people remember it. They smile. Their faces just light right up.

JANELLE: It's funny how ice cream has this natural way of serving up a smile to someone's face.

CHAPLAIN: It's true! I saw Eisenhower after the war many times. Bradley too. The Bradleys lived out here in California and attended Westwood Hills Christian Church. We'd meet after services and get together and talk about the ice cream.

After Ike was elected President I was serving as Chaplain out at March Air Force Base. Ike was hospitalized there and I went in to visit him. And guess what? He reminisced with me about the ice cream. He remembered. He smiled and all like that.

JANELLE: Maybe ice cream can help bring peace to a troubled world.

CHAPLAIN: In some ways I think it can.

JANELLE: Ice cream did a lot to build morale. What else did you think to do that would help keep spirits high?

CHAPLAIN: Yeah, a little ice cream went a long way. Candy bars too. Now I was never assigned KP duty, but once in a while some of our officers would serve the men. That did a lot to build morale.

JANELLE: And did you go into the war knowing morale-boosting was in the job description?

CHAPLAIN: I just simply knew that evil men had brainwashed the other side. We couldn't always know what they were planning. That message was clear. So I spent the war preparing God's message for the men. I did my best to bring comfort to them by praying with them, listening to them, doing all I could to help them survive and get by, always searching for ways to make them feel better.

Some men were scared. Some were sick at heart over the loss of their loved ones. Some were angry. Some felt bad about the killing. I told them all of this is forgiven by our Heavenly Father. *He knows our cause is right and just. We have to stick together in His name, for freedom, and get the job done.*

JANELLE: How important is forgiveness, do you summate?

CHAPLAIN: You know I ended the war with Patton. You know when Bradley had Patton in his office to discipline him about the incident when he slapped that soldier (There was a soldier in a hospital bed with hardly an injury. Patton thought he was an insult to the service, making a mockery of other men who were seriously wounded. When Patton visited the hospital, this soldier wouldn't get out of bed to salute, so Patton scolded and slapped him.)

Bradley made Patton stand there in silence quite a while, then he said, "George, don't ever do that again. Now go out there and do your job."

If you think about that little incident, just for a moment now, it's fair to say that *forgiveness* led to the right side winning the war.

JANELLE: Did you ever feel it could have gone either way?

CHAPLAIN: I had to keep the faith, but I saw things all the time that had me worried. Near the end of the war we captured their B2 factory. I drove my Jeep all over that factory, through great big hangars loaded with machinery they were using to make bombs. There were tunnels and assembly lines. It was very sophisticated evidence these Germans were smart people. So, yes, I think things could have turned any which way, and the war could have turned out differently.

JANELLE: Where were you towards the end of the war?

CHAPLAIN: Before the end of the war we captured Nordhausen. Just before we got there the Germans set the camp on fire. Then the Germans gave themselves up by the thousands. They were afraid of being turned over to the Russians. I think I mentioned we took good care of our prisoners, and they knew that.

Nuns and priests there came to me and begged me to help them get back to their parishes. With careful planning and thoughtful prayer, I did my best to make sure they got back to where they needed to be.

One day I was speaking in Los Angeles when a man came up to me. He looked at me and turned as white as a sheet. He said to me, "I was at Nordhausen. I was freed at Nordhausen."

JANELLE: Your contributions were so vast and so many during this war.

CHAPLAIN: These were just some of the things a chaplain had to do. I'd do it all again. I'm sure Chaplains today are prepared to do the same thing. We're in good hands.

"The Army Chaplain"

In this man's army, I believe you'll find
Oft' times a man, with a troubled mind.
Perhaps a man who wants a letter,
Written to mother that he's better,

Or that old old soldier, Joe,
Been in four months without a furlough;
Or perhaps there's one whose soul
Cries out for a more spiritual goal.

In this man's army along with these
There's one who tries their minds to ease.
Whether Catholic, Protestant or Jew,
There's something the Chaplain can always do.

Take your troubles to the Chaplain
You'll find in him a real true friend.
You are his and he is yours,
From home to Italy's bloody shores.

No you will never find his name,
In the mighty hall of fame;
But on every battle front you'll find
A Chaplain in the very front line;

Armed only with God's Holy Word
But sharper still than a two-edged sword.
And this poem stops, unfinished and undone,
Because the Chaplain's work is never done.

—Ebert Chatham
(*Written somewhere in Italy, 1942*)

III

CALLED TO DUTY

*"When God opens doors,
I go through them."*

—Chaplain Barber, June 6, 2003

ᏩᎭᏩᎭᏩᎭᏩᎭᏩᎭᏩᎭ ✦ ᎠᏉᎠᏉᎠᏉᎠᏉᎠᏉᎠᏉ

JANELLE: When did you decide to volunteer as a chaplain?

CHAPLAIN: I made up my mind to volunteer for service in 1940.

JANELLE: What prompted you?

CHAPLAIN: One day in early 1937, two young members of the Communist Party came into my office at the Park Avenue Christian Church in Montebello, California. They handed me materials bent on selling me their ideals. They were recruiting me.

We spent over an hour together. They praised all the wonderful accomplishments of communism and socialism and what it could do for the people and take the money away from the rich and people who put down other people and so on. Let's just say

I was not swayed and they did not succeed.

There is no God in communism. Communism is the most evil and destructive force in the world. There are so many problems that go along with communism. I've seen it all my life. Look at the problem of starvation. People, children, are starving to death right now while we eat our nice dinner here at Jack's.

I have worked with so many people at top levels in organizations all over the world. We've raised countless dollars to help feed the starving people of the world. Have you ever known a communist to do that? AND IT'S BECAUSE OF COMMUNISM THAT THE PROBLEM STARTED IN THE FIRST PLACE! Unfortunately, people like these young communists back in 1937, though they themselves were quite confused, they have succeeded in infecting many of our fine country's institutions.

JANELLE: A lot of "isms" have that kind of effect on a changing world. What do you suggest we do in response? Do you affiliate with any particular political party?

CHAPLAIN: Party isn't as important as how we respond, but can you guess?

JANELLE: What party? Republican.

CHAPLAIN: How did you guess?

JANELLE: Like many people, the party of your parents.

CHAPLAIN: No, my daddy was a Democrat.

JANELLE: I have a story about political guessing for you.

CHAPLAIN: Let me hear it.

JANELLE: At eight-years-old or thereabouts, I walked the streets of La Palma in a campaign for my dad. He was running for re-election to the local City Council. He was the Mayor at the time. I was pretty excited by all that so I marched door-to-door singing, "Me-n-the-Mayor, me-n-the-Mayor..." I carried pamphlets shaped like footprints that read: *Keep La Palma a Step Ahead, Vote for Hank Frese.* All I had to do was place the pamphlets in the mailboxes or through the screen doors.

I'm eight, right? I wasn't prepared to talk to anyone, so when this large smoking cartoon in a muumuu stood peering down at me from behind her screen door I grew a little bit nervous.

"What have you got there?" She asked me and took a drag off her menthol cigarette.

I mumbled something like, "Uh, I'm Janelle and my dad is," and she cut me off in mid-sentence. She continued to cough and gasp for air. I thought I'd done something to upset her. Then, in a long rusty squeak she opened the screen door and ripped a footprint pamphlet from my hands. I stood frozen in fear. Finally she garbled, "Well, is he a Democrat or a Republican?"

Now I had no idea what those words meant. I didn't know this was a non-partisan city election, or what that even meant. So I just stood there stun-gunned.

"WE-ELL?" She opened her eyes real wide and googley.

I fumbled for something to say, but babbled the repeat of, "Um. I'm Janelle, and my Dad,"

She raised her voice an octave, squinted up tight and said, "I don't care who you are. I want to know what PARTY he belongs to!"

"P-Party?" I was puzzled and ready to cry. The woman stepped down, put her cigarette out in one of those tall metal cylindrical ashtrays on her concrete porch. She put her hands to her hips and spelled out her demand, "is he a DEM-O-CRAT or a RE-PUB-LI-CAN?"

Sufficiently stumped I ventured a guess, "Uh, a Republican?"

"WELL, I'M A DEMOCRAT!" She screamed, tossed the footprint at my feet and slammed the screen door in my face.

CHAPLAIN: Oh, boy.

JANELLE: I dropped all the footprints and ran screaming all the way home. I threw myself onto the living room couch and cried into a paisley pillow, "WHAT PARTY?!"

My mom tried to help, but I resisted insisting, "Dad didn't say there was going to be a PARTY!"

CHAPLAIN:(chuckling) Oh, my goodness.

JANELLE: I still hadn't a clue what really happened on that porchfront, but I remembered, "DEM-O-CRAT!" That was enough to give me nightmares for years after.

CHAPLAIN: So you're a Republican?

JANELLE: Is that a guess?

CHAPLAIN: Thank you for that story. That's proof positive of the power of representation.

JANELLE: Meaning?

CHAPLAIN: We best be careful how we behave. See, I just might be the closest thing to the *Bible* someone ever gets to meet. I must keep that in mind at all times. Hold fast to your convictions, my dear. God knows what's in our hearts and minds. There's no deceiving God.

You know, people get confused. That woman probably had a good reason for feeling the way she did. She's just confused. With all those cigarettes she probably didn't feel very good either. There are good people everywhere no matter what affiliation they choose. Republican, Democrat, whatever, good is everywhere. People just need to be guided in the right direction and sometimes they don't have anybody to help them. That's my job. I feel good about that.

JANELLE: Do you feel it's good that we have the freedom to make our own choices?

CHAPLAIN: Absolutely. God gave us *free will* and this country was designed with that in mind. But we must work together in order to make things happen. I think our President is trying to gather as many good minds and hearts as he can in order to win this war on terrorism. And it is a war, too, not a conflict or a crime.

Democrats and Republicans alike know that, or they should. People everywhere need to understand that. In election years, they need to think carefully about that and choose wisely. Consulting God is always helpful. Our President consults God every day and I'm glad to know you consult God and choose wisely, too.

JANELLE: Thank you. That's a refreshing reminder.

CHAPLAIN: Friends should always remind each other about God and good choices. Let's pray, *We thank you, God, for Ji-neel. We are so glad to have this time together to share and to enjoy a meal and to have fellowship like this. Keep her safe and protected and her children too. We ask that you continue to bless this work we are doing and we say these things in the name of Jesus. Amen.*

JANELLE: Amen.

DEMETRIOS (OUR WAITER): AMEN!

CHAPLAIN: So, back in my office, circa 1937, after those confused communists tried their best to recruit me, I began to feel the urgings to more closely follow what was happening with the world. I have always paid attention to community and country and world events, but this experience led me to take a closer look at Washington and our statesmen. I had always been in touch with leaders, all my life, but as we grew closer toward the 1940's and the War starting, some leaders in Washington contacted me and asked, "Would you write a paper for us?"

They gave me a subject which was: *The Limit to Toleration of Alienisms in America.* So I wrote this paper for them. I covered atheism, Nazism, fascism, socialism and communism. They came back to me saying, "We like what you wrote," and went on, "you know we don't draft ministers, priests or rabbis into military service." Ministers, priests and rabbis are exempt from military service, you see. "But," they went on, "when we find someone we think can make a tremendous contribution to the nation we ask that they volunteer to become a chaplain. You are the kind of person we'd like to see serving as a chaplain." So I volunteered.

JANELLE: You were married by that time. How did Helen feel about this? You had little babies and you come home one day and say, "I'm going to join the military!"

CHAPLAIN: Well, she had mixed feelings. We both did. We'd been talking about it. We prayed together. We consulted God. My doctor had been called to active duty. When he'd come home on weekends we'd talk too. He said to me, "They need chaplains in the service. You'd be a good man for the job."

JANELLE: When exactly did you join up?

CHAPLAIN: In July of 1941, I was commissioned in the Army Reserve Program as First Lieutenant Chaplain. My orders came through on my birthday in August of that year. We were not at war yet, but we were building up.

JANELLE: Where were you living at the time?

CHAPLAIN: I was living in a little house on Greenwood that I bought for $1,700 dollars. I'll take you by there so you can get a good look at it.

I got my orders sent to that address, assigning me to the 11th Horse Cavalry. They were stationed down near El Centro.

I went out and bought myself a uniform and some other equipment. When it was time, I said *goodbye* to Helen and the boys at home. It was sad. We all cried. I got in my car and headed south. I reported for duty on October 22, 1941, before Pearl Harbor. There were some wooden buildings, but they put us up mostly in tents.

JANELLE: How were you welcomed?

CHAPLAIN: Oh, the commanding officer welcomed me graciously, "We're so glad to have you," he said. Then he got this trepid look on his face and said, "You do know that this is a horse cavalry unit?"

I said, "Yes, sir."

Then he asked me, "Have you ever ridden a horse before?"

I said, "No. No, I haven't."

He smiled and said, "Well, that's alright. Don't you worry about that. We have a horse here who's never been ridden before! You two can start out together." Sometimes the horse made the jump and I didn't, and vice versa. It was a great experience. I remember for Thanksgiving weekend I helped arrange to bring 200 of my men to Los Angeles by train. They stayed in the homes of people and were entertained in Hollywood and all like that. Guess who one of the entertainers was?

JANELLE: Bing Crosby?

CHAPLAIN: Close. Bob Hope.

JANELLE: I was on the right *Road!*

CHAPLAIN: We went back on Monday after a wonderful time. My men were from places all over the country, so this was a real special treat for them.

Then came Pearl Harbor. Who would have thought we were *On the Road* to war? Three days after Pearl Harbor we moved from El Centro to Camp Lockett, about sixty-five miles to Campo, which is on the border with Mexico. It's half-way between El Centro and San Diego, up in the mountains, right on the border. We were afraid the Japanese might try to come in through Mexico so we moved our whole camp, including horses.

I rode horseback for those sixty-five miles. I couldn't sit down for a week afterwards. The men said, "The Chaplain won his spurs on that ride!"

I started out in a tent. Then I had my own room as a Chaplain. I would room in the barracks in the Officer's Quarters. I had a cot and a table with chairs. As Chaplain, you had to have certain privacies because you'd have men needing to come in to talk to you. I had an office in the chapel, too, and sometimes somewhere else on the base. We had a nice new chapel, new buildings and places to stall our horses.

JANELLE: Who took care of your horse?

CHAPLAIN: I had an orderly who took care of my horse for me. He was sort of an assistant to me too. He also worked in the Chapel.

JANELLE: Was your family able to visit?

CHAPLAIN: Helen would come down. There wasn't room

for a family to stay in the BOQ, but there were cabins in a little mountain town about sixteen miles away. We made friends with some people there who would let her stay with them. Her father and mother, William and Louise Koester, would bring Helen and the boys down. The Koesters were of German descent. In fact, one of their grandfathers was Mayor of Berlin! They spoke German, but they had been in this country a long time.

JANELLE: My father's father was born in Germany and came to this country as a young man. He could never pronounce my name so he called me, "da girl," or his, "leedle veepa-shnappa." He hated the Nazis.

CHAPLAIN: The Koesters did too.

JANELLE: Did you get together for Christmas that year?

CHAPLAIN: Oh, at Christmas time we couldn't get out of camp, see, so they all came down and stayed in a cabin close by. On Christmas Day they brought an electric oven and why, we cooked our turkey in that oven in the Chapel on Christmas. They could come on the camp and we could eat together and share as often and as much as we could. My wife was a real good trooper and she took good care of the boys and all like that.

JANELLE: What role did the 11th Horse Cavalry Unit play in the early stages of the War?

CHAPLAIN: From there we were slated to go to the Philippines. They were using horses over in the Philippines more than we were in the United States. In preparation for that trip we had to receive inoculations for any disease we may pick up overseas. We were all given shots so we wouldn't get yellow fever. The whole regiment came down with yellow jaundice. Everybody was yellow. Faces all pallid. The good news was it saved us from going to the Philippines.

JANELLE: Where did you go instead?

CHAPLAIN: Along in the spring of 1942, why, it was decided that horses were not going to be practical in the United States for war purposes. Patton was just beginning to build his tank divisions. They transferred us and switched us to tanks. They picked us all up, except for our horses, and sent us all the way to Fort Benning, Georgia to form the 11th Armored Division.

We got down there at an interesting time. It was summer and boy was it hot and humid. I was born and reared in Georgia, but I'd been away for so long, I'd forgotten about the heat. And though I was the Chaplain, I still participated in field training. I'd run through obstacle courses and run mock battle maneuvers. I'd crawl under barbed wire, climb over high obstacles, move around hedgerows, all kinds of things. On those days I wore fatigues just like anybody else. Training days lasted mostly all day, then I'd get to go back to the barracks, shower.

One day I learned they were forming the 13th Armored Division out in California at Camp Beale. The military was trying to organize the Chaplaincy to have one chaplain for every thousand men. We ended up with fourteen chaplains and only twelve thousand men. My little ol' wheel in my pee wee brain began to turn. I thought, "Hmm, my family is in California…" So I put in for leave. They give you thirty days a year. You can take it five days at a time, or what-have-you. It depends on the situation in the military. I took fifteen days and hopped on a plane to Washington to go meet the Chief of Chaplains, William R. Arnold.(U.S. *Army, 1881-1965; ref. Study Guide.)*

What a wonderful, charismatic Catholic priest and full bird Colonel, the highest rank one could hold as a Chaplain during the War. He welcomed me graciously. We hugged and shared and prayed together. We talked and talked and talked.

He said, "We're so glad to have you in the service. I've heard about your work. You stand for the King and preach the gospel and lead people to God. Keep guiding our men the way they should go as good American soldiers."

And finally he asked me, "Why did you come to Washington?"

"I wanted to meet you," I said.

He laughed. Then I told him we had an overage of Chaplains where I was and that I'd heard about the 13th Armored Division starting up. With my family being out there and all like that. Why, I said, "I wonder if I could get a transfer to California?"

He paused for a minute and asked me, "Have you been to Washington before?"

"No, I haven't."

He said, "Why don't you go out and take a tour of the city? Come back around 3:00 this afternoon."

So I did. I took in all the sites. When I returned to his office he looked at me and he looked at his personnel man. He hollered, "Can we get the Chaplain fixed up?"

Then he looked back at me and said, "You'll have your orders when you get back to your base."

I shook his hand and turned to leave when he stopped me. He said, "Wait a minute! You haven't been to Chaplain School yet. I have a Chaplain school starting up at Harvard University."

He waylaid me and ordered me to Harvard University for three months. I thought that would be interesting. And it reminds me of a story about a man who was driving up a little countryside lane. He approached a crossroads. There he saw a little boy along the side of the road who looked like he needed a ride. The boy didn't know which way he wanted to go.

"Son, which way do I take you, to the right or to the left?"

"I don't know," said the little boy.

"Do you know where I just came from?"

"No."

"What do you know?"

"I know I'm lost," said the little boy.

"Where do you live?" the man asked.

"I live over there in that house," the little boy replied.

"Is your father home?"

"No."

"Where is he?"

"He's in prison."

"Oh!" the man was surprised, so he said, "What about your mother?"

"She's in the asylum!"

"Well, is there anyone else in the family?"

The little boy said, "My brother."

"Where is he?"

"He is at Harvard University."

The man was so intrigued, "Oh, tell me what he is studying."

The little boy said to the man, "He ain't studyin' nothin', they're studyin' him!"

So the Chief hooked me up to Harvard, but I still had fourteen days left of leave. I saluted the Chief and went out to grab a taxi. We hurried to Andrews Air Force Base. I walked up to the operations desk and asked the officer there,"Have you got anything going out to California?"

He said, "Catch the Lieutenant walking out there."

I rushed out and said, "How about taking a chaplain to California?"

He said,"Grab your bags, Chaplain, and let's go!" We boarded a C47, like a DC3, an old two engine plane. Douglas made 'em. The C47 was to the Air Corps what a half-ton truck was to the Army in those days. They didn't fly by night, so we had to land in Dayton, Ohio, and get up early the next morning to continue our trip to the West.

I sat in the co-pilot's seat. The pilot said, "Chaplain, have you ever flown one of these things?"

I said, "No."

He said, "Well, you drive an automobile, right?" and he showed me a few things, *Pull up when you want to go up and push down on the stick when you want to go down or turn to the right when you want to go right, left, and so on. Focus your eyes on up ahead a few miles away. Fly even.*

I took over the flight and flew it three hours. He was amazed. He said, "Oh, boy!" I didn't tell him that the first time I had ever been in a plane was the day before when I flew to Washington!

JANELLE: You didn't land the plane?

CHAPLAIN: No. He did. We eventually landed in Burbank. My wife, Helen, was staying with her folks. I took a taxi over to their house in Montebello. When I got there and I knocked, my little three-year-old greeted me saying, "Daddy! Daddy!" but he did that to every soldier who came to the door and Helen didn't come. She just stayed in the kitchen thinking it was just another soldier. I stood at the door and waited. When my wife finally recognized me she was so surprised. She'd thought I was in Georgia. We had a nice time together. I said to them, "We are all going to Boston!"

JANELLE: I remember my dad taking us all to Twenty-Nine Palms when he was on active duty with the Marine Corps.

CHAPLAIN: Let me hear about that.

JANELLE: It was during the summer months, each summer for a few years. I was little. This started when I was two-years-old or so. During the long car rides I annoyed everyone. I kept busy by bouncing and babbling in the backseat. But when we approached the main gate at the base I'd stop whatever I was doing so I could see the *salute*. I'd say, "Daddy! Daddy! That man is gonna *fa-lute* us!"

When our 'Bug came to a full and complete stop, I climbed onto my dad's lap to get a better look at the guard at the gate. I'd watch his automatronic arm rise up to form a sideways vee. I'd study my dad's likewise response. It made me deeply curious. After passing through the gate I'd ask what they were doing back there. Dad said they were just saying, *"Hi."*

At some point over those summers the main gate salutes became what I called, "Hi-Falutin'!" I do believe that soldier's salute served to symbolize my writing heart's journey.

CHAPLAIN: (chuckling) You should write a story about that, and call it *Hi-Falutin'* too!

JANELLE: Maybe I will.

CHAPLAIN: I think you should, could be a calling.

JANELLE: Now tell me how you finished out your final days of leave.

CHAPLAIN: After thirteen wonderful days with my family,

I went back to Burbank with my travel orders and caught a direct flight to Fort Benning. I packed up my stuff and picked up my car.

JANELLE: What were you driving?

CHAPLAIN: I had a Chrysler automobile and I drove it to Boston to settle in for Chaplain School. I decided I would get a little apartment or something there. I brought Helen and little Russ Jr. back to Harvard with me. Don stayed with Bup and Gram (*Koester*). They loved him so, and he loved them. Everybody had a nice time while I attended Harvard.

JANELLE: Do you remember any of the other Chaplains you attended school with?

CHAPLAIN: Two of the Chaplains that went down on the Dorchester were in the same class with me. The Jewish Chaplain, Rabbi Alexander Goode, and the Methodist Chaplain, Rev. Clark V. Pohling, they were two of the four Chaplains on board the Dorchester.

JANELLE: What happened to the Dorchester?

CHAPLAIN: In 1943, The Dorchester took a deadly hit. The Chaplains knew the ship was going to go down so they gave their life vests to four enlisted men, locked arms, and went down with their ship. I have a friend who is writing that story for film. *The Four Chaplains* had their calling and now my friend found his by telling the world about it.

JANELLE: Why hasn't anyone else approached you for your book project?

CHAPLAIN: Because God chose you.

JANELLE: You mean this is my calling?

CHAPLAIN: *When God calls us to action, we must answer that call and persevere.* Ji-neel, I know you'll turn this out right.

JANELLE: This is out-right frightening for me. I've never written a book before.

CHAPLAIN: And I'd never ridden a horse before! Have faith. I believe in you. You have to believe in you too.

JANELLE: I have faith, but I also have a loud, annoying critic inside my head who heckles me all the time.

CHAPLAIN: Listen to the voice inside your heart. That's where Jesus lives. Hear Him calling to you.

JANELLE: Did you learn to encourage like that at Harvard?

CHAPLAIN: My faith is built from years of experience, but Harvard's Chaplain School turned us all out right.

JANELLE: After Harvard, where did you go?

CHAPLAIN: Several of us Chaplains finished up our experience speaking at various churches. Some of us spoke all the way up into New York. They all respect you if you've been to Chaplain School. Then I charged up that Chrysler and got ready to cross the country again. I found my tires weren't too good. I went down to the O.K. Tires in Washington. The man in charge was having some personal problems and I just happened to be there to help. I listened and I prayed with him. After, he said, "Give the Chaplain a set of four new tires!"

So we set off for the drive, but took our time. We had Russ Jr. We only drove 250 miles a day, seeing all the wonderful sites along the way. I think every American ought to see these great things all across our great land.

JANELLE: I think it should be a prerequisite for citizenship.

CHAPLAIN: Maybe voting too.

JANELLE: That's a great idea.

CHAPLAIN: Maybe make people take a test before they vote.

JANELLE: Wouldn't that be telling? That would boil down to who writes the test.

CHAPLAIN: True.

JANELLE: So you ended up back in California at Camp Beale?

CHAPLAIN: Yes, it was going on 1943. We were working there to build tanks for the 13th Armored Division. I can proudly say I helped build two tank divisions for Patton!

I was the Protestant Chaplain there at Beale. I held services for my men in the Chapel every Sunday, and of course spoke at many of the churches in the whole area there. I preached at churches in Sacramento, Marysville, and Yuba City. I brought my family up to live in Yuba City for a while. We also had a Catholic Chaplain. I don't remember if we had a Jewish Chaplain, but I remember we took good care of our Jewish soldiers too.

Not long ago, I was down in downtown Los Angeles when I ran into one of my Jewish soldiers from Camp Beale. He was in civilian clothes and I was too, but he recognized me. He said, "I know you. You got me leave for all my holidays!"

One day at Camp Beale, the General called me and said, "We've got a regiment of fifteen hundred black troops serving over at Herlong, California, in an ammunition depot (Sierra Army Depot)." It was about 60 miles north of Reno, Nevada. The General went on, "I was asked to send them a Chaplain to guide them and help them out. I would like to know if you would be willing to go on detached service for two or three months."

JANELLE: Herlong is out in the middle of nowhere.

CHAPLAIN: I gladly volunteered for that. After all, a General was asking. But you're right. We were out in the middle of nowhere, not much to do. I called on the Red Cross to see if they could furnish me someone to help. They sent me a wonderful little black lady. She was a graduate of Columbia University. She did so much to help my men out there. The two of us put our minds together and came up with some pretty good ideas.

My men would often go to Reno to gamble. The gambling element didn't like them to be there. I didn't like them going down there either. One day I went and visited all the gambling places in Reno and said, "You know what? I know you don't want my men in your places, and the military doesn't want them in there either. How about we help each other out here. I'd like to build them a recreation facility on the base and furnish it."

They said, "Alright, Chaplain," and they gave me $5,000 dollars. I took one of the large mess halls and converted it to a fine rec' center. We got music boxes, pool tables, exercise equipment, card tables.

I also recognized a tremendous talent in those men. I decided I'd help them form baseball teams, boxing clubs, basketball teams, all the while guiding them and counseling them along spiritual lines. I felt this was one of the best works of service I could do, dealing with the whole person, the whole life experience.

This grew to our hosting programs for various clubs and organizations around the area. Our teams would play other teams. We even played the prison teams. We put on a bond rally one time and I furnished all the entertainment. We sold over a million and three-quarters worth of dollars in bonds that night.

One day it occurred to me that someday we would be going overseas. I found out that many of my men here didn't know how to swim. I went to the municipal pool in Susanville and said, "These men may go overseas and they need to know how to swim. Please open up your pool so we can teach these men how to swim," and they agreed to do that. I went to Reno and bought 243 pairs of swim trunks and we taught those men how to swim. This was 1943, several years before military integration.

JANELLE: Did any of those men have to go overseas?

CHAPLAIN: Yes. Later on during the War, I met some of those men over in Holland. They were cooks. They welcomed me and cooked me a big juicy steak. They said they had a black Chaplain serving them who was good but, they said, "We wish we had you back, Chaplain Barber."

JANELLE: Were you serving at Herlong, for long?

CHAPLAIN: From Herlong, I went back to Camp Beale for a bit. Then I was transferred to Fort Ord for a few months before being transferred down to Camp Cook (Vandenberg). I served with the Artillery for these assignments. In early January of 1944, I received my orders to go overseas. I sailed on the *Queen Mary*. For four days we zigzagged our way to the Firth of Clyde, Scotland. We had nearly 15,000 troops on board with 500 WACS. I often say in my speeches that became known as "the sugar shortage" of the *Queen Mary*.

During that trip we didn't have a Jewish chaplain with us. I was asked if I would hold services for all the Jewish personnel. They had a special chapel set aside for them on ship. If you go see the *Queen*, you'll find it's still there. So I held the first service, but they couldn't all get in. A wonderful cantor was there from New York who helped me, and I gave the sermon. It was so crowded we stayed over and held a second service so all the men could hear me. We held two services Friday night. Then on Sunday morning I held one of the big Protestant services up in the dining hall.

JANELLE: Which division were you listed with?

CHAPLAIN: I was assigned to the 1st Infantry Division. The Big Red One, that was slated to spearhead the invasion on the beaches of Normandy. We moved around the small towns in England until making our way to smaller ships to prepare for the landing on Omaha Beach on D-Day.

*   *   *

Before I met Chaplain Barber, I had a series of visions and dreams, meditations that only now I can begin to understand. One arrived in the early hours of the morning after my grandfather died.

I had fallen asleep to imagine I was a little girl giggling again. *I sat flat on Grandpa's lap as he puffed on his pipe and blew smiling white 'O' rings into the air. They invited me to follow them out into dreamlit skies.*

My spirit-self soaring, I saw the old Mission and its park across the street. There long ago, I'd played near a weeping willow. Under that big teary tree I fell to my knees.

Leaves blew in the breeze clearing to bring into view a tall man walking softly toward me. He wore a uniform shaded in blues with shiny black shoes gleaming in dreambeams. I reached out to him. He sat down beside me and took my hands in his.

In my hands he placed a book which bore a silver cross on its cover. Together, our hands wrapped around it tightly, we carried the book to cool waters rippling in a nearby stream. Standing side-by-side, knee deep in nature's baptismal channel, we watched as flowing water brought this book bubbling to life.

After this dream I awakened to write.

IV

FOUNDATIONS

*"The Bible has been known to stop a bullet,
but that's not the only reason I believe."*

—Chaplain Barber,
November 11, 2003

ᚢᚱᚢᚱᚢᚱᚢᚱᚢᚱᚢᚱ ✦ ᚾᚢᚾᚢᚾᚢᚾᚢᚾᚢᚾᚢ

The day after we met at *Jack's* for the first interview, Chaplain Barber invited me to attend a Veterans' event at the Crystal Cathedral. I gladly accepted and penned the event in my date book. In the early stages of the book's development I felt it was important to spend as much time as possible with Chaplain Barber. Especially formidable were our forays through his beloved environment, the uplifting world of patriotic Christian America.

Whenever he invited, *"Would you like to take that in?"* I tried my best to oblige. I swear if my name had been *Jack* instead of *Janelle* I'd be Trade Commissioner by now. By minding the master in me I learned to multi-task with savvy. I juggled a full-time job, dealt with divorce, developed single-parenting skills, fine tuned first-time home-buying and first-time home-demolishing, all the while collecting the data for this book which took me several dozens of places with the Chaplain across Orange and Los Angeles Counties. My house is still a mess, but I like to think of it as the *best mess.*

Always in a rush I found myself underdressed for some events, overdressed at others. I remained doubly blessed, regardless, as I always learned something new and got a kick out of watching the Chaplain enjoying himself.

He always complimented me, "*You look fantastic,*" no matter what I wore while he dressed his best in his favorite Air Force uniform. I was proud to move through any crowd on his arm. He made special efforts to introduce me, "*This is Ji-neel and she's writing my book!*"

I never called him *George* or *Russell*, only "*Chaplain*," simply because I liked to say it. Maybe the same reason he said, "*Ji-neel*," instead of something else. This true Georgia gentleman made himself easy to like. He treated me like a special lady, opening doors and pulling strings.

We attended the *Humanitarian of the Year Awards* in the summer of our first year. To thank me for driving, he took me to dinner. Outside Newport's *Oyster's Restaurant* he made a point to be the proper escort, insisting he walk streetside along the sidewalk, "*just in case.*"

There were discouraging moments. Driving along in my *sin* SUV to Bob Schuler's *Crystal Cathedral* we made our maiden voyage, engaging in the most detailed and thought-provoking conversation yet. Both hands on the wheel meant no writing, and all my eleven-dollar tape recorder turned out were car noises and ear-piercing throat clearings. The amateur in me had arrived in horrifying full force. Most of what I'd recorded to memory I jotted down in my journal later, but the vibrancy of being there faded to blank page. I was heartbroken and embarrassed.

Chaplain Barber, on the other hand, was not worried about my disappointments in the least bit. He emphasized, *"I know what I've been up to all my life, and I can tell it as many times as you like."*

For our next road adventure, I came better prepared with a state-of-the-art headset and microphone device that promised static-free recording. Chaplain Barber kindly agreed to wear the contraption and began, *"Testing, one-two-three,"* before I'd even put the cassette tape in the player. He tapped on the mouthpiece with his finger, *"Is this thing on?"*

"Chaplain, we're ready for launch," I checked his seatbelt as we rolled out of Whittier Downs Mobile Home Park destined for Supervisor Mike Antonovich's birthday party. Red light changed to green. I pressed *Record* and prompted the Chaplain to tell me his life story, again.

"Let's roll," he said.

* * *

CHAPLAIN: I was born at a little country crossroads about fifty miles from Atlanta, Georgia, called Buckhead. I was born at home probably with a midwife helping my mother. My mother nursed me. She loved me and took care of me and raised me.

JANELLE: When is your birthday?

CHAPLAIN: August the 26th, 1914. I'm the older of two children. I have one sister, Agnes. She's just about a year younger than me. At some point we moved to Atlanta. We lived near Grant Park. I don't have a birth certificate, but when I was fifteen years old in 1930, the Census taker said there was, "a fifteen-year-old boy living on Cameron Street in

Atlanta, Georgia." That's how I am able to get my passport because I don't have a live birth certificate. I don't think my sister has a birth certificate either.

JANELLE: When my daughters were born they were each given a social security number along with their official birth certificate.

CHAPLAIN: It's creepy, but it sure makes everything convenient.

JANELLE: What was your mother's name?

CHAPLAIN: My mother is Ara Bowman. She was kind of heavy set, probably 175 pounds, and sweet as she could be. She was the oldest of nine children in the Bowman family. She trained as a practical nurse and she worked and lived in people's homes for two or three weeks each month. She also took in ironing and washing. During the Depression days you had to take whatever work you could get.

My daddy was born in Atlanta, probably at home too. Jesse Oliver Barber. He was eleven years older than my mother. They got married when my mother was twenty-years-old and he was thirty-one. He trained as a carpenter and became skilled as a cabinet maker. He was also a musician, a banjo player, and he could play the guitar and juice harp. And he was a champion swimmer in Atlanta. He won all kinds of awards. I think he smoked a little bit and he chewed tobacco, too. In 1918, when they were having this flu epidemic, they came along and vaccinated everybody. When they vaccinated him he slapped a wad of tobacco over the shot so he later had to be vaccinated again.

Daddy took some kind of lick on the head as a young man, and his family believed this caused him to have a temper. He would drink, and one drink would set him off. He would become violent. He'd fight at the drop of a hat. All it took was somebody saying something, he'd curse them out and he'd fight. I don't know if he ever hit my mother. He may have.

He worked hard and made good money. He'd get paid on Saturday morning, but on the way home he'd take a turn and stop at the pool hall. One drink and he'd start to gamble. He wouldn't come home until late. By then, the money'd be gone. He tried to be good to us. He _was_ good to us. He was a good man. He loved me and my sister and later in life when he got over his drinking, he lived to be about eighty-five years old.

JANELLE: There's longevity in the genes.

CHAPLAIN: Right, yeah, right. I'm eighty-seven, and I still have so much to do.

JANELLE: Was religion part of your parents' plan for you?

CHAPLAIN: Daddy was a member of the Christian Church. My mother was a member of the Baptist Church. I was baptized in the Baptist Church when I was nine years old. Daddy didn't go to church with us though. My mother raised me in the Church. The greatest gift she gave me was bringing me into that church. She opened me up to that whole experience which has helped me all through life.

She always took me to church, even on a weekday evening and every Sunday morning. I loved my Sunday School teachers and the preachers in our church. I learned the Bible stories from Genesis to Revelation. I treasure those stories.

So I grew up walking closely with Christ and the church, and also I learned to love people and how to relate to people.

When the evangelists would come hold a revival meeting, my mother'd take me. They'd come and hold large meetings two or three times a month. I'd sit and listen in those meetings where an evangelist preacher would teach about Jesus Christ and the gospel. My heart was touched by that so much it caused me to develop a great respect for the great preachers and spiritual leaders of America. So early on I learned about the love of Christ, the church *He* established, and the power of preaching.

At one evening meeting, I was about nine, I began to cry. My mother took me down to the front where the preacher was and she told him about my crying. He said I was having, "an experience," and they immediately voted me into the church. I got baptized right there.

My mother said to me, "Unless you are baptized in the Baptist Church, you are not done right." Most down in the South think unless you are a Baptist or Methodist, *you done been tampered with.*

I was baptized *In the Name of the Father, and the Son, and the Holy Spirit* right there, backwards into the water, in my street clothes. I got all soaking wet.

JANELLE: What was your mother's reaction?

CHAPLAIN: She was crying too, with a sweet happy smile on her face.

JANELLE: I was nine when I was baptized.

CHAPLAIN: How about that! Did your mother take you?

JANELLE: Yes she did. I was under her spiritual guidance like you were with your mother.

CHAPLAIN: Which church was that?

JANELLE: I was baptized in the Congregational Christian Church of Huntington Park in California. This was the church my grandparents helped develop. My grandmother designed the stained glass windows and my grandfather was in charge of foundations. At my baptism, he was seated there next to my parents. Right before I bent over backwards and got dunked in the water, I caught a glimpse of him. He was crying.

CHAPLAIN: Did you cry too?

JANELLE: Yes, but my tears blended in well with the waters below.

CHAPLAIN: Don't be ashamed to cry. Baptism makes everybody cry. Tears of joy and *Alleluia!* Did you keep attending church regularly after that?

JANELLE: No. We sort of moved around from church to church.

CHAPLAIN: Oh, I see. You know I was close to my grandfather and he was my mother's father too, Grandpa Bowman. He wore a straw hat. He was a small man about five feet tall. Scotch-Irish decent. My grandmother was a quarter Cherokee. She was only fourteen when she married him. When I was a little boy of about five or six I used to go down to my grandfather's cotton farm out in the country and pick cotton. I'd pick a hundred pounds in a day.

JANELLE: Didn't that hurt your little hands?

CHAPLAIN: Sure, sometimes, but he'd pay me and there were lots of folks there helping. His farm was over a hundred acres. Everybody picked cotton. Grandfather, Grandmother, Father, Mother. We had black people that worked in the home and cleaned the house. They worked with us too, and got paid. They loved us kids. We had lots of fun on the farm together. The cotton would grow up and the bulbs would open. We'd pick the cotton out of the bulbs and use it to make cloth - there are machines for that now. Mom used to sew for us. She made all my clothes- I wore short pants most of the time. I didn't have a suit until I graduated from Jr. High.

JANELLE: Where did you attend school?

CHAPLAIN: I went to Hoke Jr. High School in Atlanta there.

JANELLE: Whatever became of that cotton farm?

CHAPLAIN: At one time, in the 1920's, Grandpa Bowman was worth a hundred thousand dollars. Back then that was a lot of money. Then the boweevils came and destroyed the cotton farm. He was reduced to poverty.

JANELLE: Did the family recover?

CHAPLAIN: Spiritually we were fine, but we remained poor. Church was a big mediator. The rich and the poor alike can attend together, and all in between. God does not discriminate.

JANELLE: Did you always live in Georgia?

CHAPLAIN: No, we moved to Florida in 1925 I think it was. We lived there for four years or so, until 1929.

JANELLE: After your baptism, did you attend church regularly?

CHAPLAIN: Yes. I attended regularly and in my young life, I had Christian Endeavor every Saturday evening and before Sunday service. There is where I first learned to speak about Christ and associate with all sorts of other young people. Almost all churches across America have similar youth groups, and in those programs you hear missionaries tell their stories and hear of their work with other people in other parts of the world. I learned about the little children all over the world who were hungry, starving. That gripped my heart and soul, you see.

So we would take up an offering and give it to those missionaries. Sometimes we'd send some to the missionaries wherever they were across the world. We did this so we could help these children to satisfy their hunger, or get clean water and shelter or love, and education too. Of course, we also hoped they would come to know Christ. Everybody in the world has these basic needs, especially the world's children.

JANELLE: On the back of your business card these things are printed. You've got *LOVE, Hope, Food, Water, Health, Shelter, Education, Peace, Security* and,

CHAPLAIN: *Freedom!* That's right. And not particularly in that order every time. Those building blocks make up my mission: *To make everyone I meet aware of the basic needs of every human being, to help them understand how accessible these things can be if we learn to serve one another, provide for one another.* Give a dollar. Serve. Join one of the many fine organizations we have across America. Encourage each other to build up the proper foundations for living, for everyone.

JANELLE: You make it sound so easy.

CHAPLAIN: Politics removed, it is.

JANELLE: Don't forget all the *"isms."*

CHAPLAIN: That's what I'm talking about.

JANELLE: If you could rewrite your paper today, would you add or change anything about it?

CHAPLAIN: I'd heighten the *limit of toleration* on those alienisms. I'd also add *terrorism* to the list of -isms that need eradicating.

JANELLE: Amen.

CHAPLAIN: *Amen* indeed.

JANELLE: But, if I am sheltered, without hope or love or education or any of these good things that you have listed on the back of your card, or if I am confused, what can I do? Where can I go?

CHAPLAIN: Run to your nearest good Christian missionary. Walk with a preacher. Talk with a teacher. Seek out a veteran

who will tell you the truth. There are many many good people in the world who understand these things. There are good statesmen. Seek them out. Talk and listen and learn. Let God live in your heart so you may discern right from wrong. Let your God-given intuition help you to know the truth when you hear it. And change the channel or outright turn the TV off.

JANELLE: What a coincidence. I'm practicing *media deprivation* all this week for my night class assignment.

CHAPLAIN: What's that?

JANELLE: No TV. No newspaper or magazines. No radio. No nothing. I'm keeping tuned in only to my God-given intuition. I'm writing. I'm spending more quality time with my children. It's great. Challenging, but great.

CHAPLAIN: What a good idea. But don't forget to keep informed of what's <u>really</u> going on in the world. Keep tuned into God.

JANELLE: I'm developing the knack for weeding out what my drama students call, "whack," so I can get down to what is real.

CHAPLAIN: Good for you. Keep it up. Do you know where we are going? I think I'm lost. Maybe you know better than I do where we are going.

The tape had more time on it, but we had arrived at our destination. Cause to pause. The Chaplain insisted I hang his handicapped placard from my rearview mirror so we might cut the walking distance from car to party. After the event, we drove back to Whittier through Montebello...

CHAPLAIN: Where were we?

JANELLE: Lost in *Love* and *Hope* and *Food* and *Water*...

CHAPLAIN: Right, yeah, the back of my business card. I give out thousands of cards a year. You saw me tonight. I tell everybody good news and give them a card. If people read my card, they might understand it has a message. So with this trust and love for Christ and for the people of the world, especially the little children of the world, I developed a desire to preach the gospel and to become a minister.

I remember one summer, our church had a camp for young people. It was held in Tacoho Falls, Georgia. That was my first experience in summer youth camp. I was fourteen. Summer youth camps have since become a regular experience for most Christian churches. I helped develop one out here in California, *Angeles Crest Christian Camp*. What a great place that is for our young people today. Like many campers, I attended my week-long camp about the same time I entered high school.

JANELLE: Where did you go to high school?

CHAPLAIN: I went to Tech High School in Atlanta, Georgia.

JANELLE: Tell me about your school life.

CHAPLAIN: I had wonderful teachers. I also took ROTC, Reserve Officer Training Command. One of the reasons for that was they furnished me with a uniform. We were poor and that uniform helped me to have some clothes to wear to school. We trained from 7:30 in the morning until 8:30, before school.

That gave me some military background which eventually led to my service as Chaplain.

I graduated from high school in two-and-a-half years. Typically, it was a three-year experience for students, but I finished all my work early in January and went through mid-year graduation. I wore my uniform. That was 1932. I was offered a scholarship to Emory University in Atlanta, Georgia. I was good at math and science, so it was an academic scholarship.

Well, the next day after I graduated I was downtown visiting my friend Woody Perry's sister. She was in our church. Woody had gone to Cincinnati Christian College the year before and he was home visiting. Roy Davis was there too, he'd gone on to that same school.

JANELLE: What church did you attend together?

CHAPLAIN: Grant Park Christian Church. Roy had come home for a funeral and we just happened to meet downtown there. As we talked he said, "Russ, why don't you come with me to Cincinnati?" I told him I'd just graduated the night before from high school and all like that. But as we talked, Christ seemed to say to me, "Russ, go to Cincinnati." So I finally said, "Why not?" and I went home and told my mother.

JANELLE: What did she think? You had a scholarship to Emory and everything.

CHAPLAIN: And Emory is a good school. It's where former President Carter has his program now. But, oh, my mother was very supportive. She said, "Son, I'm just so delighted for you. If that's what you want to do," and so on. I packed up some clothes, my Bible and things. I had two dollars and five cents in my pocket! We took off in a Model A Ford, 'drove from Atlanta to Cincinnati. I started my Christian ministry and college education there, on $2.05.

JANELLE: What type of degree did you earn?

CHAPLAIN: I earned my bachelors degree. On the very same day I earned my bachelors degree, I gave up my bachelorhood! I married Helen Koester of Cincinnati on June 11, 1936.

We then set out for our honeymoon, a three-month cross-country adventure to California.

We arrived in California and took a hotel, downtown in Los Angeles. We had breakfast in a restaurant there and bought one of those big, thick, chocolate malt milkshakes, for ten cents in 1936.

We went out to the Tomlinson's home near USC. He was the pastor of the University Christian Church not too far from the USC campus. Mr. Tomlinson's daughter and Helen were about the same age and were the best of friends. He had been the pastor of their church in Cincinnati. He took a church out here in Inglewood before moving to the University Christian Church.

JANELLE: Who was the man who married you in Cincinnati?

CHAPLAIN: That was John Wilson. Let me tell you about the day he married us. You see you had to have a special permit, not just be a minister of a church at that time, in order to perform weddings. John was a new young preacher and he got that permit in the morning of June 11th. Then he married us that evening!

JANELLE: Where was the wedding ceremony held?

CHAPLAIN: In the Columbia Avenue Christian Church there in Cincinnati, Ohio. Ruben Anderson was the minister. They were all connected with Cincinnati Christian College where I was studying for the ministry. If John Wilson hadn't received his license, well, Ruben Anderson would have had to sign the official papers. But John signed them. He just retired from a very successful ministry in Springfield, Ohio. Like me, he trained lots of young people for the ministry and missionary work all over the country and all over the world. He just finished publishing his book called *A Vessel Molded and Used by the Potter*. Isn't that a nice title?

JANELLE: It's great you are both still in touch.

CHAPLAIN: He's an amazing man. I'll always stay in touch with him. I like to keep in touch with so many good people all over the world.

JANELLE: After he married you, how did you and Helen make your way out to California?

CHAPLAIN: In a black, two-door Ford V-8, one of the first V-8's that came out in 1936. It was a good car. Of course it didn't have air conditioning. We eventually bought some kind of makeshift contraption that you'd hook onto the window like this here and we'd fill it with water. The air from outside would blow in. It was not as satisfactory as the air conditioning you've got running in this nice Ford *Expedition*. This feels good.

JANELLE: I wonder what Henry Ford would think about the evolution of his automobile.

CHAPLAIN: That makes me wonder what God thinks about the evolution of man.

JANELLE: That's a packed thought to ponder.

CHAPLAIN: Ponder. I like people to ponder.

JANELLE: When exactly did your motor trek west conclude?

CHAPLAIN: We arrived out here in July. I was ordained at the University Christian Church. Here's how it worked: In our churches, the leaders of the local churches—the elders and deacons—are the ones who ordain the ministers. We're not ordained from some headquarters. The local church is the highest body of Christ's kingdom. That's what we believe.

Very soon after I was ordained, Brother Tomlinson took his vacation for most of the month of August. I found through the years that most preachers took their vacations during the month of August for some reason or another. Brother Tomlinson asked me to preach the four Sundays that he was to be on vacation that year, which I did.

JANELLE: This was 1936. A new beginning.

CHAPLAIN: Correct. Now, Brother Tomlinson had a great reputation. In his ministries, he never missed a Sunday having additions to the church, either by confession of faith and by baptism or by transfer of membership from one Christian church to another. I carried on that tradition. I went out and called on the people and the visitors. Every Sunday I had additions too.

Brother Tomlinson was such a great preacher. He never had a note. He memorized the scriptures and his sermon and his poetry, everything. Never a turn to anything, never afraid, he'd just stand up there and go. I followed that pattern myself for the first ten years of my ministry out here. Even today I can just stand up and preach a sermon and quote my scriptures.

JANELLE: What happened after Brother Tomlinson came back from vacation?

CHAPLAIN: While I was preaching that August in 1936, the elders and leaders of the Park Avenue Christian Church in Montebello came over to hear me two or three times. They invited Helen and me to come over on the first Sunday in September to preach at their Montebello church. We did.

We preached morning and evening. The elders said, "We've listened to Brother Barber at the University Church. We've talked to him a lot and now he's free. We recommend him and we call him to be the minister of the Park Avenue Christian Church." Everybody voted for me, all twenty-five of them in the congregation! Democratic ruling you know. The elders and deacons, everybody, like Christ had established in the Bible.

JANELLE: Twenty-five? That's it? Why such a small parish?

CHAPLAIN: The church on Park Avenue was a real discouraged bunch. They had just lost the parsonage, the house next door. They were broke and couldn't make the payments. They owed about everybody in town. Gas, electric, water. So it was a very sad situation that needed rescuing. But God knows all about those things and He called me, a young man to serve who didn't know that it couldn't be done.

I was willing. I was on fire in preaching the gospel and I knew my Bible pretty well. I knew how to build a church some. I began to preach the sermons and the church began to grow.

JANELLE: You were that "someone" who had to re-lay the foundation, give it a re-attunement.

CHAPLAIN: That was my calling.

JANELLE: Besides preaching what did you do?

CHAPLAIN: One of the first things I did was set aside time every day to go out and visit the homes of the people in town. Every day I'd walk up and knock on a door. A lady or somebody would come to the door and I'd say, "I'm Russell Barber. I'm the new minister at the Park Avenue Christian Church. I just wanted to know you."

If they gave me an opportunity, I'd continue. I'd say, "If you don't go to church anywhere we invite you to ours. We'd like you to come to our church." If they'd invite me I'd say, "I'd like to step inside the door and have a short prayer in your home here." They'd usually say, "Fine, come on in."

JANELLE: What prayer would you present?

CHAPLAIN: I prayed for the people in their home that *God's blessing would be upon them each one.* If they had a special need that God would help in their need, and in the *Name of Jesus Christ*. I'd leave after that and go to the next door.

I called on every home in Montebello. There were only about 5,000 people living there at that time. I don't know how many homes that would be, but I called on every home in Montebello over the next three months. That paid off because through the years people would meet me on the street and say, "You're the only preacher who prayed in my home."

JANELLE: Did it work? Did the congregation grow significantly?

CHAPLAIN: It took months and months, but I believe I brought that Church up from twenty-five discouraged members to nearly seven hundred truly inspired people. Christ-loving and all like that.

JANELLE: That's quite an accomplishment.

CHAPLAIN: God was at work in me. Everybody has that potential. You like baseball. *If you build it they will come.*

JANELLE: Churches everywhere are integral parts of their community. Team members.

CHAPLAIN: That's right. And they should be. That goes for all churches, all denominations, all religions. The people who joined the Park Avenue family certainly did their part to build that city of Montebello. It was a winning team and they are still doing good things.

JANELLE: Were you the bullpen or the bench?

CHAPLAIN: I was the bullpen catcher who warmed everybody up. Helen was my cheerleader.

JANELLE: I bet nobody kicked dirt over home plate on your watch.

CHAPLAIN: That's right. It's a shame our President can't say the same.

Chaplain Barber called a timeout to show me a few of his stats, sites in the city along our drive. He shared with me bits of city history. He talked about his chaplaincy with the Montebello Police Department.

His community service pertained not only to church parishioners, but spread to counseling patrol officers, doctors, lawyers, teachers, community leaders, mothers, fathers, teens, even babies, as well as passers by. He never met a stranger. Everyone was, "*Friend.*"

His call to duty demanded he tend a blessed blend of fatherhood, neighborhood, and holy brotherhood, many times in army boots. As we drove down the streets of his sacred old stomping grounds, twilight flashbacks rolling by, I heard him say so softly and mellow,

"*I helped build the city of Montebello.*"

V

DENOMINATIONS

"For where
two or three come together in my name, there
am I with them."

—Matthew 18:20

It was Sunday and we were not in church. Instead we were sitting in our thoughtful spot, the corner booth at *Jack's Salad Bowl*. Chaplain Barber prayed for us. I asked him, "Is it okay for us to work here on Sunday when we haven't been to church?"

"This is church," he said, "*...wherever two or more come together in His name, there He'll be sitting among us.*"

"So God approves?" I queried.

"I think so. I suppose we'll know for sure if we get struck by lightning or not."

"I hope not."

"Don't you worry about a thing, Ji-neel. This is wonderful to be here with you today. You can count on Christ to send us His love and blessings all afternoon."

"Chaplain, your faith inspires."

"*Amen* to that. Now what will you be having today? The ham looks good," the Chaplain checked the senior special.

I closed my menu. "I think I'll stick to my regular B-L-T today."

"Sounds good," he said. "I think I'll have that too. Great minds think alike."

LUNCHABLE TAPE...

JANELLE: As Chaplain, did it matter which denomination you claimed?

CHAPLAIN: No, but I'm a Protestant. The Christian Church. Disciples of Christ. A Christian. *I'm not the only Christian, just a Christian only!* You know Jesus didn't establish any denominations. He established a *church*. And the church is <u>not</u> a building. People made church buildings for their own conveniences. Christ walked all over the place and people gathered outside, inside, wherever they could. People have become their church, and people have argued for centuries about *who's right?* and *who's wrong?* and *which church is true?* and *who's not?* It's spun nearly out of control. That's why you have to keep it simple today. Get back to the basics.

JANELLE: What are the basics?

CHAPLAIN: What Jesus taught, *Love the Lord your God completely and love your neighbor as yourself.* Living with these two basic principles can only cause you to do right.

JANELLE: Is there any way for people to understand this and get over the argument?

CHAPLAIN: Maybe. If they understand what they're getting by doing right.

JANELLE: What will they be getting?

CHAPLAIN: The gifts of the Holy Spirit: Love, joy, kindness, peace, goodness...I've never known anyone to throw free gifts away, have you? No church has split over the gifts of the Holy Spirit. One of the reasons the whole world doesn't believe is because of all the divisions we've created, quarreling back and forth. I don't quarrel with anyone. I just try to lead people back to a simpler understanding of what Jesus taught from the beginning. I try to keep things simple, not social or political, though I do have my leanings.

JANELLE: Is this evangelism?

CHAPLAIN: Just practicality.

JANELLE: Is there a preacher today you can identify this with?

CHAPLAIN: Billy Graham. Billy Graham's program is evangelistic. I say he is the greatest living evangelist since the apostle Paul. There's power in every prayer. I have worked and lived with some of the greatest spiritual leaders around the world, and Billy is one of the greatest in the world today.

JANELLE: I get confused by all the titles and styles a preacher takes. I never quite understood the differences between, say, *Pastor* and *Minister*, or *Reverend* and *Father*. What name or title do you most associate with?

CHAPLAIN: I liked it when Helen called me her *darling*

Russ! And I like to be associated with Christ.

JANELLE: I guessed that, but can you...?

CHAPLAIN: I can address that. In church, it just became *Pastor* or *Minister*. Between church members, we called each other *Brother* or *Sister So-and-So*. I never liked *Reverend*. The word *reverend* should only be used to describe God and we don't believe in elevating men to the status of God. That is why I never chose to be called *Reverend*, never-ever *Reverend*.

JANELLE: When you were serving in the military, what did *your men* call you?

CHAPLAIN: Early on they said, *Chaplain, Sir,* sometimes *Captain* or whatever my rank was at the time. Mostly, *Chaplain*. During the Vietnam War, serving as Wing Chaplain with the 452nd, they called me *Padre*. No matter what they called me, I answered. I was Russell as a boy, or Russ. My full name is George Russell Barber, but in the military when you drop the middle name I went by George R. Barber. I'd say, "Sir," to the officers.

JANELLE: If it doesn't matter what they call us and it doesn't matter what specific church we choose to attend, why can't we all get along?

CHAPLAIN: I think it all boils down to experience. I had an *experience* when I was very young. You read about things like that all the time. A light shines down on somebody or somebody dies and comes back. Someone has a vision. You have your dreams and meditations. Whatever the case, after this *experience*, somehow some way, a deeper understanding begins to grow. Love begins to happen. And God is love. Once love conquers the heart, good things happen.

JANELLE: What if someone goes through life never having an experience?

CHAPLAIN: That's where we fit in. We share and bear our testimonies so that others can understand.

JANELLE: How can anyone know the heart of another man he hasn't bothered to understand?

CHAPLAIN: We do our best.

JANELLE: Integrity.

CHAPLAIN: Right. We show up, keep our word, bring in *The Word*. We try to bring the *good news* to everybody we meet. God's news is good news.

JANELLE: 'God *with an extra 'O' in it*.

CHAPLAIN: And, <u>oh</u>, doesn't it feel good to do good? Maybe that's another gift you get when you do God's work.

JANELLE: Service to others.

CHAPLAIN: Serving others is serving God. Now you know why I always recite verse from Matthew 25, "...*whatever you did for one of the least of these...you did for me*," (from Matthew 25:40)

JANELLE: Is creating also serving God?

CHAPLAIN: Sure. Look in *Genesis* where so many examples of creation are given.

JANELLE: God's power source.

CHAPLAIN: But what are you getting at?

JANELLE: Together, you and I are creating this written work.

CHAPLAIN: I see.

JANELLE: This book project is *an experience* in, and of, itself. Through the commitment to the work, we are also creating fellowship, a lasting friendship, which is love.

CHAPLAIN: And God is love.

JANELLE: Could it also be God's loving wish that we do what we love?

CHAPLAIN: Tell me what you're thinking.

JANELLE: I went to Unity Church in Anaheim one Sunday where the message was *God loves being me.* We were guided to meditate on those words and that concept.

CHAPLAIN: That's very positive. I'd like to go there with you sometime. I know that Christ wants us to know Him. Everything he taught was love. So why not?

JANELLE: We've been to many Christian church gatherings together, of various denominations.

CHAPLAIN: Right, and they all delivered a good message about God's undying love for each one of us. Didn't you get that message and get recharged?

JANELLE: Every time, with Jesus more than Master Teacher, the Savior in the center. But for each individual I think God's message of love can take on many different meanings and reach people at many different levels.

CHAPLAIN: That's true. That adds to the meaning of *experience*. Everybody has to experience for him or herself God's message in order to know what next to do. Then, you do what is right. When you do what's right, it feels right. I'm sure God would be happy for you when you are feeling happy. And that's alright.

JANELLE: A *holy communion* of the spirit.

CHAPLAIN: Or your definition of synchronicity.

JANELLE: Isn't it interesting, Chaplain, we were both baptized when we were nine? That's synchronicity in our lives.

CHAPLAIN: Tell me about your church-going experiences.

JANELLE: I've had a few.

CHAPLAIN: Who baptized you?

JANELLE: *Reverend* Fred Sevier, in severely cold water. He was a kind and gentle man. My grandfather loved him very much. He served the church my grandparents helped finance and build.

CHAPLAIN: The one in Huntington Park?

JANELLE: It isn't there anymore. I think the Salvation Army runs a charity out of the old buildings and offices. I have one of the old hymnals.

CHAPLAIN: Do you remember having any spiritual or

emotional experiences?

JANELLE: I learned to play the *Steeple People* game. I was very emotional about that.

CHAPLAIN: What is it?

JANELLE: You lock your hands together like this and you say, "Here's the Church," then you put your fore fingers together to a point and say, "Here's the Steeple," then you open your interlocked hands at the base of the thumbs and say, "Open the door," and you separate your palms, "WHERE'S ALL THE PEOPLE?" Then you do it again, repeat it all, with your fingers inside and say,

CHAPLAIN: Like this, "HERE'S ALL THE PEOPLE!" Isn't that cute? I know that one.

JANELLE: My grandmother taught my mom when she was a little girl. My mom taught me.

CHAPLAIN: I bet you have taught little Marlena and Mikayla how that goes too. That's a good tradition to keep handing down.

JANELLE: No pun intended?

CHAPLAIN: God has a sense of humor too. Where do you think ours came from? Even the littlest of tiny babies laugh. Tiny babies come directly from God. They may know his language best.

JANELLE: I've often thought about that. Sometimes I've thought of my personal relationship with Christ as being childlike, "Me and the Laughing Jesus."

CHAPLAIN: That's okay! However you get the message, as long as you get His message. Did you go to Sunday School too?

JANELLE: I just remember crying a lot. When I was little-little, before being baptized, I was always demanding I remain on Dad's lap or holding Grandpa's hand. I wanted to sit with the Steeple People and sing.

CHAPLAIN: What songs did you sing?

JANELLE: I remember singing "Onward, Christian Soldiers" for some strange reason.

CHAPLAIN: That's interesting.

JANELLE: Did you also sing that one?

CHAPLAIN: We probably sang it in my church too. But did you know this hymn was sung at the funeral of President Dwight Eisenhower at the National Cathedral in Washington D.C.? That was March of 1969.

JANELLE: I was two.

CHAPLAIN: That's something. This here hymn is taking me back. Now did your little church have accompaniment? Did someone play an organ?

JANELLE: There was a sweet lady who played the piano.

CHAPLAIN: Helen played a little piano. We also had a nice lady who ran our music program. She was very talented and could play and play and play. Ida Crumb. Ida Crumb was no crumb, though, she was the whole loaf!

JANELLE: And, Chaplain, you are the *Little Big Man* of

the *Greatest Generation.* I can just see you now, singing in the church. Did you enjoy church hymns?

CHAPLAIN: Oh, they're my favorite songs. I love them all.

JANELLE: Promise me you won't be offended if I tell you how we sang "Onward, Christian Soldiers"?

CHAPLAIN: Of course.

JANELLE: You know how the song goes, right?

CHAPLAIN: (singing) *Onward, Christian sol-diers, marching as to war, with the cross of Je-sus, going on before...*

JANELLE: That's the one. I can blame my brother for this. We were kids so we sang it *LOUD-ly,* exaggerating and emphasizing every syllable. We didn't know we were singing the wrong words, (singing) *ON-WORD, CHRISTIAN SOL-DIERS, MARCHING OFF TO-WARDS THE CROSS-EYED JEE-ZUSS! Going on before,* and we'd fade into humming, *hmm...hmm...hmm.*

CHAPLAIN: That's hilarious! Kids can get away with that. Don't worry about that. Jesus said, "*...unless you become as a little child, you cannot enter the kingdom of Heaven...*" By that he meant we must develop that childlike faith, that trust and belief in Christ without reservation, for Jesus also said, "*... suffer the little children to come unto me for theirs is the kingdom of Heaven...*"

Every little child is innocent without sin until that child comes to the age of accountability and he deliberately chooses to follow either right or wrong. We must all become like little children, trusting, if we are to enter the kingdom of Heaven.

JANELLE: That was the very first verse I read at Crossroads Youth Group.

CHAPLAIN: Where was that?

JANELLE: In Buena Park there was a little Community Christian Church I attended on Tuesday nights. I was the little drummer girl in the inspirational Christian rock band. I wasn't really little. I was a teenager. I played a big black *Rogers* drum set. I still have it. Our lead singer was a guy named Happy. We thought we were good, but we weren't very inspirational. We got busted for playing secular music and they fired us.

CHAPLAIN: Misguided, that's all.

JANELLE: It still brought me to Christ. *"It's Tuesday night! Welcome to Crossroads!"* I'd break into a vicious drum rhythm and we'd start jamming for Christ in our hearts. Everywhere I went I found Christ. In college there was Fellowship of Christian Athletes.

CHAPLAIN: That's a great group.

JANELLE: I also attended the LDS church.

CHAPLAIN: You followed the *Book of Mormon*?

JANELLE: There was a lot to read, tons of supplemental reading material, but they taught mainly from the *Bible* first. I was baptized again, this time by my uncle, who is an active member, on what would have been my grandfather's ninetieth birthday. It was beautiful, very spiritual.

CHAPLAIN: But you didn't stay with it?

JANELLE: I was impressed with their focus on the importance of family. My girls and I needed that nurturing after the divorce. And I love family history. I'm still very interested in genealogy. I found a long, lost relative just the other day.

CHAPLAIN: Who?

JANELLE: My grandmother's youngest brother, Harry Lindgren. He served aboard the USS Saratoga CV3 as an aviation ordinance officer during the war. He died tragically in 1946.

CHAPLAIN: What happened to him?

JANELLE: He was on a bus on his way to Los Angeles from Washington D.C. to visit everybody out here, family. Apparently, he was suffering from Post Traumatic Stress Disorder, undiagnosed, and in a panic the bus driver let him off the bus in the middle of the desert. There he wandered alone and lost. Several weeks went by before his remains were found. My grandfather kept a detailed record of all the family's efforts to find Harry and sort out the fallout so Harry's immediate family would be cared for. He left a young wife and two tiny girls behind.

CHAPLAIN: Unbelievably tragic. War does crazy things. It's a shame no one diagnosed your great uncle's illness. But you can rest assured that he is taken care of now. He's with the Lord in Heaven and I'm sure he is proud of you.

JANELLE: I see him sometimes in my dreams. I get a little

slice of *Harry Heaven* from time to time.

CHAPLAIN: You know, you are so thoughtful, and you've had so many spiritual experiences. Your spiritual quest is most interesting to me.

JANELLE: Would you believe I also attended the Russian Orthodox Church? I taught Sunday School at the Hollywood parish and went to worship services almost every Sunday. The Orthodox tradition honored my first baptism, so I didn't have to partake in another one, but I went through a three-day spiritual cleansing process called holy Chrismation. The priests there were very spiritual men, good leaders. The girls were both Christened there. I liked the namesakes we were given.

CHAPLAIN: When was this?

JANELLE: This was when I was still married and the girls were tiny.

CHAPLAIN: Why aren't you married anymore?

JANELLE: I guess you can say two worlds collided. Children were created. After that we drifted apart, like the continents. Earth.

CHAPLAIN: It's too bad I'm not thirty years younger and you aren't twenty years older. I'd marry you. We'd be perfect for each other.

JANELLE: Wow!

CHAPLAIN: We need companionship. God did not intend for us to live alone. You won't be alone forever, Ji-neel.

Somebody will come along and sweep you off your feet. He'll be a good man with a good heart. You'll teach him to know God.

JANELLE: Are you a psychic?

CHAPLAIN: I just know that we are meant to have a partner in life, and you, especially, deserve a good one. You mentioned the importance of family. I subscribe to Dr. Dobson's *Focus on the Family*. I know him and his teachings are good. I'll see to it you get a copy of that magazine.

JANELLE: Thank you. I'll read it, but I'm fine. I don't mind being a single mother. It's not a negative plight. In the power of my now, I have my place and there is still God's *presence and power and peace*.

CHAPLAIN: But you deserve better. Who's the girls' father?

JANELLE: His name is Igor.

CHAPLAIN: Igor? 'sounds Russian.

JANELLE: He is. That's what led to my finding the Orthodoxy.

CHAPLAIN: How'd you meet him?

JANELLE: At a wedding reception. Foreshadowing! He was the entertainment. He's quite a talented musician. He composes and plays in a Russian folk music group called *LIMPOPO*.

CHAPLAIN: Poo-po? What? How old is he? Was he in the Red Army? Is he a communist?

JANELLE: Limpopo, it's a river in Africa. He's my age, and

yes, he served, if you count playing trombone in the band being communist.

CHAPLAIN: The communist influence is very dangerous. I hope he is a Godly man.

JANELLE: The girls love him.

CHAPLAIN: He needs to be a good father to them. Shall we pray for him?

JANELLE: Sure, why not?

CHAPLAIN: Tell me why you stopped going to that first little church that baptized you and what made you wander.

JANELLE: Too many tears. After my grandmother died, it became too difficult for our family to attend. I always missed it. I still miss the steeple people and the little things like our singing, or my dad's lip-syncing. He didn't like to sing, but he'd pretend most vivaciously.

CHAPLAIN: Funny.

JANELLE: You know what else I miss about our old church?

CHAPLAIN: What's that?

JANELLE: I miss the smell of old lady perfume.

CHAPLAIN: There's plenty of that here in *Jack's* today!

JANELLE: I miss the powder room and holy communion served with *Saltine* cracker-bits and thimbles filled with *Welch's* concord grape juice.

CHAPLAIN: I like these trips down Memory Lane. Now tell me, how did your grandmother die?

JANELLE: That's a long left turn.

CHAPLAIN: I've got time.

JANELLE: Her case is still unsolved.

CHAPLAIN: She was killed?

JANELLE: Yes. Her murder has haunted us for decades.

CHAPLAIN: Oh, no, that's just terrible.

JANELLE: It tore to the core and left our family bruised and battered. Tender hearts shattered. She was everywhere in that church. Her love and energy inside every stained glass window. Her time and talent in every *Tinsel Tea* church fundraiser. I still have one of the toys she made, a raggedy old quilted cat with a tail of yarn.

CHAPLAIN: What was your grandmother's name?

JANELLE: Theone.

CHAPLAIN: What's that? Spell it.

JANELLE: T-H-E-O-N-E, like THE ONE, only pronounced, *Thee-Own*. She was by name, "The one and only." It's my middle name too. I carry her with me in my "T". My cousin and I passed her name on to our kids as well.

CHAPLAIN: Keep tradition alive!

JANELLE: I do my best.

CHAPLAIN: This was your special grandfather's wife? On your mother's side?

JANELLE: Yes.

CHAPLAIN: You knew your grandfather's pain. I knew the pain of my grandfathers too. We are symbiotic in that way.

JANELLE: My grandfather spent the rest of his life, in his own way, trying to make sense of her death, trying to keep the family close by keeping traditions alive.

CHAPLAIN: That's hard to do without a matriarch.

JANELLE: My mother still tries to fill those shoes, but she especially knows things were never the same.

CHAPLAIN: It's incredible the impact one act of violence can have on an entire family, an entire people.

JANELLE: "Somehow, some way, some good must come from this," were my grandfather's words to the family. To me he said, "Good is God, with an extra 'O' in it."

CHAPLAIN: Good words to live by. How old were you?

JANELLE: I wasn't quite five years old when that happened. I've been searching for her ever since, and documenting it in my writing all my life.

CHAPLAIN: You could write another book about all that.

JANELLE: We have to finish this one first, Chaplain. Sometimes I feel like I'm never going to finish this book.

CHAPLAIN: Well, let's think about that for a moment.

You know, we've talked about forgiveness. Remember when Bradley forgave Patton? Remember the power of that?

JANELLE: Yes.

CHAPLAIN: After you ask God to forgive you, no matter what you think you've done, you have to forgive yourself too. We are here to do good things, no matter how long it takes. I've got time. There's no pressure. You're doing fine, just fine. We're trying to cram almost ninety years into this package, so we have to take our time.

JANELLE: I know, but sometimes I get stuck in novice mode, and that's when my annoying inner critic begins to bark back at me.

CHAPLAIN: Don't ever doubt yourself. You wear the Armor of God too, you know. You are protected and the Lord will see you through this. Let's pray. Let's pray right now for you and for Theone and her baby brother, Harry, and for your grandfather who's gone on to meet them, and also for your girls and their father, for your mother and father, "*Our Father in Heaven…*"

* * *

Sometimes I tried too hard to write this. Those were the days my head got stuck in tomorrow. I stressed myself silly over time and time again. Deadlines, self-induced deadlines, lack-of-time excuses, or the new spin on deadline because of aging and fear of death. Fears of final farewells ran frantic through my mind, especially on fuzzy up-too-late writing nights.

If *what-if's* ever worried me to weeping, I dialed up Chaplain

Barber, the *Bishop of Jack's Salad Bowl,* my personal Jesus. He always awakened for my call, quickly taking me on a walk with all God's promises, gentle prayers that brought me back to breathing easy.

One delightful drizzly evening, while driving home from a night class, I fell to happy pieces. Laughing, crying, trying to make sense out of the puzzling purpose of this project. I had an epiphany, *an experience.* In the moment, I called the Chaplain from my crackling cell phone. The conversation coasted me along in the rain.

"Chaplain," I said, "I think I've figured it all out, why we've been working together these past many months, why this book is so important."

"Okay," I heard him smile from the end of his line. It didn't matter I woke him up.

"Who are we to each other?" I asked flatly, matter-of-factly.

"Huh?" He coughed.

"It's because of what my buddy, Isabelle, said in class tonight."

"Who? What's that? Hello?"

"Chaplain, can you hear me?" I flicked the phone.

"I can hear you now."

"It's because you are important to me and I am important to you. My friend, Isabelle, with big Carol Channing eyes said, '*Being important to someone else is the answer to all your truth– seeking questions,*'" I stated in my cyber dialect amidst cell phone static.

He cleared his throat ready to speak, "That's probably true."

I diatribed, "Isn't being important to someone else all about making life meaningful? Isn't this your purpose, your gift? Your life has had such great importance to countless others."

The Chaplain chimed in chuckling, "You know, you're just

wonderful!"

I continued waxing, "All those you've served during wars and in peace, Chaplain, they counted on you for their hope and strength. Your congregation longed for your message, their lifeline in troubled times. Your friends, YOUR FAMILY, all the strangers -I know you've never met a stranger- but everyone who came seeking to hear you speaking, and your *Bibles*, your little pocket Bibles, well, Chaplain, this is all so important," I babbled on, "It's like the flowering essence for living a meaningful life."

"You're so right," he agreed. "Everything we do is important. All those experiences mean so much. You're important too!"

"How about a book entitled, *It's a Meaningful Life?*"

He laughed and lauded, "GOD BLESS JI-NEEL!" A gorgeous giggly smile spread across my face when I heard him say my name like that. It tasted better than ice cream. He continued in prayer, "And God bless her girls, her mom and dad too, keep her safe on her drive home." He digressed, "Is it raining out there?"

"Just a little bit," I answered.

"You be careful driving in the rain, in the dark and all like that."

"Oh, I am. You're right. I should really get off the phone. But I just had to tell you while it was all fresh in my mind."

"That's alright, Ji-neel. You can call me anytime you want, day or night." My phone began to break us apart just when he began to drop names. I heard something about, *"Mrs. Peale,"* calling earlier. I thought about her husband, Norman Vincent, and his power of positive thinking. Important. Important to each other.

The Chaplain's voice morphed to Morse code on, "Co-lin Po-well...Am-er-i-ca...Pro-mise..." Though intrigued, I became completely lost in communication space. The conversation cued for an open conclusion. I said, "I'm so glad we had this chance to talk tonight."

"Me too, Dear." He cheered me, "HURRAY, JI-NEEL!"

"O Chaplain! My Chaplain!" I re-prosed patriotically.

"Goodnight. Keep in close contact now. Call me tomorrow."

Into his, "*Sweet dreams*," my phone fainted. I flipped it closed and found my way to the freeway, new deep thoughts driving me home in soft rain sparkling in the night lights.

Chaplain, it's a certainty we're the same denomination.

VI

SERVICE STATIONS

"For I was hungry and you gave me something to eat, I was thirsty and you gave me something to drink, I was a stranger and you invited me in,"

—Matthew 25:25

ᏩᎳᏩᎳᏩᎳᏩᎳᏩᎳᏩᎳ ✝ ᎠᏫᎠᏫᎠᏫᎠᏫᎠᏫᎠᏫ

Chaplain Barber practices what he preaches when he encourages people to pay attention. He says he keeps tuned in to world events and national news on an hourly basis. *"Hour of Power!* I watch it every evening. I keep in close contact with Washington too. I got *Fox News* on right here."

After the President spoke directly to him, via live public television broadcast, the Chaplain took it personally to heed the call to all veterans. "The President wants us to go out to the schools and speak to as many children as possible during the month of November."

The Chaplain's translation of the President's speech led me to the notion I could design a school forum for him. What better experience for a kid to hear about D-Day than directly from someone who survived? I invited him to speak at my alternative high school, and my daughters booked him for their elementary classes as well.

I'm not certain where his influence will stop, if at all. The impact he made on these two distinct groups of public school kids is still being talked about. Children of all ages fell under the spell of his personal history. In his presence they were empowered, proud to have a piece of him. Most will admit they were left resting assured there is hope for peace in their world some day.

Gabby, a troubled young girl who later earned her diploma with honors after a long, arduous trek toward graduation, wrote for the campus newspaper after experiencing Chaplain Barber's rare-form visit:

GILBERT GUMBIES SOBER UP, GET G.I. HIGH

Every day is just like any other day at my school where we all suffer from the pains of childhood, cancerous grades and the open sores of social defeat. Our school colors are black and blue, appropriate symbolism for where we've been and what we've been through.

Then one day, my teacher brought Colonel Chaplain George Russell Barber to school to speak to us in celebration of Veterans' Day. I heard from the student rumor mill it almost didn't happen, his message of service almost banned due to dangers of a religious nature. If this one day had escaped us or left us behind, like every other day, several souls, including mine, may have gone unfed. Thankfully, on November 15, 2001, a few handfuls of us chose to accept the invitation to hear Chaplain Barber speak in the faculty lounge, our only forum for visitors at the time.

He came to tell us about his experiences at war and in life. He told us about himself, and yes, he has been working in Christian ministry for seventy years and serving as a chaplain sixty years. He is the last living U.S. chaplain who landed on Omaha Beach, the bloodiest beach in Normandy on D-Day. It makes me sick to think I almost missed this living legend who chose me and my peers for his audience, the normally uninterested, alternative teens of today. He did it gladly and for free.

Chaplain Barber began his talk by sharing about his military service that began in October, 1941, before Pearl Harbor. He was with the 11th Horse Cavalry Unit. At this point in his speech, he humored us with a story about having never ridden a horse before.

In 1943, Colonel Chaplain Barber, then Captain Barber, served with 1500 black troops in Nevada. He had fun with them and they played games together. When he found out that they didn't know how to swim, he went out and bought them all swim trunks and taught them how to swim. This all took place before the Civil Rights Movement and Integration.

Chaplain Barber shared with us a personal experience about the Queen Mary, or the "Grey Ghost" as the ship was called during the war. On board with him were over 15,000 men (and later 500 WACS), heading into preparations for D-Day. He performed services for both Protestants and Jews on this voyage. In 1996, if it wasn't for Chaplain Barber's help to stop the Queen Mary from being sold and sent to Japan, who knows if it would be here today!

Chaplain Barber told us about Ernie Pyle who walked the beach after D-Day and saw the destruction, "he picked up a little Bible... he walked around with it for a while, then he set it back down on the beach..."

As he told us that story he held up a pocket Bible and presented it to a teacher from our staff. Frozen in awe, she accepted it with respect and gratitude.

Chaplain Barber told us about serving ice cream in what became *known as the "best mess" in England. He said that ice cream was remembered by Generals Eisenhower, Bradley and Montgomery.*

During the march across France and Germany, Chaplain Barber was in General Patton's unit. After the Remaugen Bridge collapsed, he held two of his men in his arms as they died. He was the only chaplain at the bridge at the time and his name went around the world.

He told us when he was in Seoul, Korea, during the Korean War, he helped save 56,000 orphaned children. When he came back he also helped build up March Air Force Base, the largest air wing in America.

Chaplain Barber simply served others wherever he was during World War II and he continues to serve others today. He ended his visit by telling us he would be honored to serve in this war against the terrorists. He said we could help too. When one of my classmates asked him to tell us how we can help, he suggested we each send a dollar to the starving children in Afghanistan. He said the children of America have already raised over one million dollars for them. He encouraged us, "Serve wherever you are. Serve, and help others."

His comments left us feeling hopeful and a little bit safer and more secure, "We are winning this war. We are on God's side, the right side."

It certainly felt okay to hear "God" that day, especially so soon after September 11th. As I was leaving the room, I turned to look back. Chaplain Barber was holding up two fingers on each hand, the signs for peace and for victory.

Gabby made a good choice the day she lumbered into the lounge for the life lesson. She will surely remain one of the impassioned, empowered to pass along a piece of history that resonates love, not hate. Service without strings. Good things to keep in life's back pocket.

As she continues her walk through life I pray she remembers the day she wrote her article about the Chaplain's visit. Hers is a voice that speaks volumes. Her pen to paper is a proud, loud and clear understanding of the importance of service.

Later on in the course of our commitment to the President's public service announcement, Chaplain Barber spoke to my daughter's third grade class. Mikayla prepared a precious message of introduction and read it quietly in front of her classmates in Room 19:

"Hello, my name is Mikayla. I would like you to meet a very special friend of mine. He is a veteran from World War II, and a very important part of our American history. My mom is helping him write a book about his life story. He is here today to tell us a little bit about his life in celebration of Veterans' Day. Please welcome my friend, Colonel Chaplain Barber."

After energetic criss-cross applesauce applause, Chaplain Barber jumped to his beginning, "How many of you have ever ridden a horse before?" Growing hands shot up like little rockets. He entertained them with their favorite treat, "How many of you like ice cream?"

Mikayla's class sang in a chorus, "Oh me, oh me!" Their room was an electric rainbow of color and origin. Twenty-eight charmed children sitting at the feet of the dapper chaplain-in-a-chair.

"Do any of you like to dance?" He told them about Bob Hope and the USO. They gazed bug-eyed. From their square spaces on the classroom carpet they laughed, listened, glistening in learning about a life of history and the world they will inherit in swift due time.

A sampling of what they wrote to the Chaplain after his visit reflects the memories that will most likely live on unforgotten:

"Everyone was quiet when you were telling us about the war. It takes a lot to keep us quiet."

—Jillian

"Thank you for going through so much trouble for our country. You must care about us. I bet that took a lot of practice."

—Taylor

"This was my luckiest day ever in my whole life. I never got to see a real super-duper hero come to our school before. I learned so much I told my parents and my little brother on Veteran's Day."

—Fay

"I can't wait for your book to come out because I want my mom to buy it."

—Alisha

"Thank you for telling us about the big mess you made."

—Arthur

"It would have been so sad if they didn't get any ice cream."

—Alice

"I think that I am with you on praying and caring for children all over the world."

—Christian

"I was so proud to meet you I almost fell over."

—Daniel

"Thank you for telling us the story about the kids who don't get presents for Christmas. Maybe I'll donate some presents this year and decorate them with pretty bows on top."

—Ronald

"Colonel Barber, you dress very neat. I like that about you."

—Eric

"You are a very nice person. When I meet you again, let's have some ice cream."

—Shawn

Third grade couldn't have been more mesmerized. The Chaplain thanked the kids kindly for welcoming him and asked them to thank their teacher for allowing him time to visit. He promised them they were the best kids he'd ever met and told them to tell their parents they were doing a good job, raising them up right.

The kids mob-moved the Chaplain out the door with cheer, but not before he insisted on giving the teacher another souvenir from the taboo bag of pocket Bibles he asked me to bring. The little Bibles had camouflage covers, matching many public school teachers of today.

The veteran teacher politely smiled, doing all she could to publicly resist, but in her own silent defiant trust in God, she pocketed the Book anyway. God bless her. God bless teachers. God bless all teachers, fond and dear, and God bless public school.

* * *

On the way to Whittier one foggy evening, I rammed my car into the side of another. No one was hurt, but it was my fault. My car sustained so much damage it could barely crawl to safety to the service station on the corner. I had never been in a car accident before. I wasn't prepared for the body aches, the belly-aches, the deductible rates or the delay of game it would generate. I thought about Patton. The last days of Patton. Fate or faith?

I would have to learn to forgive myself. Weeks went by. Day after day without visits with the Chaplain. Not until after the New Year was my car finally ship-shaped and ready for open highway travel again. While the girls and I had a hint of holiday left before school started in January, we spontaneously planned a pick-up trip to take the Chaplain to *Jack's*.

His house was a mess. "The best mess!" he declared. Leaning towers of newspapers, copies and cut-outs filled the living room. The dining room table, a concentration camp of Xeroxed copies, spilled over and spread across floor. He had been saving everything, "just in case."

"It looks like a war zone in here," I suggested we clean but became confused. The more I tried to strategize, the more the room seemed to move zombified. The magazines multiplied. He was overwhelmed too, but somehow he knew where everything was.

Making headway like my own infantry division I moved in on the kitchen. There I discovered decaying milk-carton corpses and an emergency ward in the fridge. Dying donuts moaned in agony, motioning for help alongside meals on wheelchair wheels. While I poked around peeking, I caught the Chaplain sneaking in the cupboard to find M&M's for the girls.

He distracted me pointing, "Take that box over there. Go through it and see if anything in there might add to my story. See whatever else you might like."

It was a box of used books, old letters and tiny treasures with my dog tags on it, *FOR JINEEL.* He motioned for me to look for more paperphenalia to add to my box.

Caught in the melee I managed, "Chaplain, this is ridiculous. How can you find anything?"

"My friend, E.V. Hill, used to say, '*I don't have a filing system. I have a PILING system.*' I use one too, you see!"

"Yeah, but look there, you've got papers on the stove top. That's dangerous." I removed the immediate fire hazard and scanned the scene for more dangers before he stopped me.

"Oh, let's go to lunch. You girls ready?"

I never argued with the Chaplain, something my God-given instinct guided me into agreement with. I carried my box dutifully to the back of my car, buckled in the children and came back for him. "Do you want me to get your mail?" I shouted to him.

"No, my mail will be just as good after we get back." He closed his screen door behind him. He was moving slower than before, slouching more too. Time at his house ticked louder in my head. *Jack's* would relieve the pressure.

Back in our booth we both felt better. B-L-T's around-the-house with banana pudding for dessert. He asked the girls how school was going. They jinxed, "Good," and sipped their lemon sodas to hide the lie.

I asked him what he thought about private school and whether or not he recommended it over public. Before I could collect his wisdom he insisted I tell him all about the car accident and what he could do to help. I still had the *best mess* in mind, wanting for better ways to serve him.

"What can I do to help you?" he asked.

"Nothing," I said, "Car's fixed. We're fine. Merry Christmas!"

I gave him his past due card and the girls drew him pictures on their paper napkins. He gave them each a crisp $5 with chocolate gold coins on top, then he continued on me. He persisted, pressing me on my finances, trying hard to make me accept help.

He insisted, "I want to help you."

"No way," I refused.

Finally he forced a check into my hand and said, "You do whatever you like with this. Reimburse yourself for the accident. Buy the girls some school clothes. Fix up the house."

Then it dawned on me we had never talked money before. This entire project was being funded from our fondness for each other and the love and kindness in our sentimental ol' hearts. We never kept score. I didn't record mileage. I never saved receipts. This wasn't a business deal with a signed and binding contract.

Receiving a personal check from the Chaplain, $500 dollars, was a wave of surprise washing over me. I wanted to deny it, especially after seeing the changes he'd endured in those few long weeks without us.

The girls got bright ideas. My nine-year-old suggested, "Why don't you use it for the book?" and my six-year-old added, "Buy some more M&M's. We need them for our mission."

I challenged, "Chaplain, you can't afford this." Saying that frustrated me further, hurling me into hysterical thoughts of how our nation neglects its veterans. I pursed my lips.

"Neither can you!" he matched me. He was right. I had to think-tank another tactic. "Where will we be going next, Chaplain?" I shifted gears.

"Next week on Thursday evening, I'd like to take you to a meeting in Altadena. I'll speak there. You can bring your camera and video and all like that. The girls are welcome to come too."

I dotted my date book and redirected, "What if I keep this check? I can use it as a visual aid. It will be a money-motivator for finishing our manuscript." In articulating an outcome for the very first time, I felt free. Only God would have thought the jarring of a car crash would cause me to see the light, not just in the Chaplain's eyes or in my children on their mission from God, but at the end of the tunnel that was turning our lives around.

"That'll be fine," he agreed. "You might want to think about private school for the girls too. This could be a down payment for that as well. The Baptists have issued a call to all parents to put their children in private school so they can get back to the basics of what a good education is all about, Bible first."

"That's interesting," I said. I committed to keeping the check pinned to my bulletin board until the book would make its demands known. This served us well.

"Thank you, Chaplain."

"Things happen for a reason," he said, "and when you understand that, you'll see the silver lining."

ON THE WAY TO ALTADENA...

JANELLE: When did you begin volunteering as a public speaker?

CHAPLAIN: Well, I've been speaking freely all my life. But sometime around the 50th anniversary of the D-Day landings a call went out for survivors. Of the Omaha Beach chaplains, I was the only one who responded. That led me to believe I was the last living chaplain from the D-Day landings at Omaha Beach. Jay Leno hosted a show in 1994 that honored the D-Day veterans and I was there. Rosie The Riveter was on that show too.

JANELLE: Did that show prompt you to participate in more public speaking endeavors?

CHAPLAIN: My family taped some oral history, and we contacted a few local papers. After a few news articles circulated around town so did word that I was available to speak. I didn't mind that at all. Some news networks have since come out to do little stories on me. You saw the video of the *KTLA* broadcast.

JANELLE: Yes, but I'm curious to know what you get out of this publicity. Don't you donate your time?

CHAPLAIN: Sure. It's all part of service you see. I speak for free, but someone there makes sure I get a ride and a meal. I get to share with people, meet people. It all works out.

JANELLE: Do you enjoy it?

CHAPLAIN: Very much. I just wish I'd get more time sometimes. I did get a check once, by surprise. I was flying to Washington D.C. for the President's inauguration. Someone on the plane told one of the stewardesses who I was and all like that. Soon the co-pilot came on and told everyone on board, "We have a celebrity with us today!" That felt good. Lots of folks were thrilled. Another passenger came over and introduced herself. She invited me to speak for her little group there in Washington, at a nice hotel. I spoke and shared all my stories. I later got a check in the mail from her for a $1,000! It came at the right time too.

Usually I'm slated to say a simple prayer these days or give the invocation. But I have so much to offer, you know? If they give me an hour I can fill it. If they gave me a day I'd fill that too. If they give me five minutes, I try to stretch it so I can help people as much as possible.

JANELLE: So your speaking is really a public service.

CHAPLAIN: That's right.

JANELLE: Don't you think you deserve to be compensated for your time?

CHAPLAIN: Well, I am in a lot of other ways. We get to have this conversation right now. Fellowship and prayer. We get to enjoy a nice meal. We get to meet new people and old friends alike. In small subtle ways it's a slice of Heaven.

AT THE SLICE–OF–HEAVEN GATHERING IN ALTADENA…

The Chaplain was welcomed warmly with hugs and happy handshakes from his old friends. This was a charity fundraiser hosted by a veterans group in which he felt he belonged. He introduced me while we moved in the flowing stream of registered dinner guests.

When we took our seats near the center of the sparsely attended room, a smiling retired Air Force pilot gave greetings and the invocation. After the Pledge of Allegiance he began the brief introduction of the Chaplain he'd known for more than a number of years.

The Chaplain rose slowly posing for flash pictures with his hands held high in victory signs. Tables full of cheer and tinking water glasses quaked and quivered in the reverie. Being in the public eye, no matter the size of this crowd, delighted him. His blue eyes sparkled. He winked at me and moseyed on up to the microphone.

He opened with, "Well, with an introduction like that, I am most anxious to hear what I have to say!"

The crowd clapped and hooted *hoorays*. Old couples cuddled closer. Little ladies who sat in the back leaned in trying to hear him better. Some scooted chairs around to face him.

He held them all in the palms of his hands, "You know, seeing a crowd like this makes me think we ought to do something religious."

A hush fell over the room. His flock sat still and remained silent while he packed his punch. He paused. Then, in self-confident crescendo, he delivered the uproarious blow, "LIKE TAKE UP A COLLECTION!"

Riotous laughter caused the black-tied waiters to jiggle their water jars. They smiled and nodded their heads trying not to spill. Chaplain Barber continued, "We could collect it and give it to your chairman here to distribute wisely for your good cause. You know you are all just wonderful and I am so glad to be here tonight…"

He closed the near hour-long program with a prayer sending blessings untold to each and every one, "I hope and pray that my life and experiences will grip your heart and soul so that you will love God and Christ and give your life in love and service to others."

That night I made polite converstion with veterans from all our foreign wars. Patriotic Americans of all ranks, shapes, sizes and ages. They were proud to know the Chaplain and were very interested in his book. I spent a lengthy bit of time with a Korean War veteran who traded me a homemade bottle of wine for my promise to send him a book when it was completed. Like fine wine, this veteran respectfully agreed, "All in good time."

On the trip back to Whittier, we stopped for gas at a Chevron service station. The Chaplain offered to buy my fuel, but I had already slid my card through the slot. "Next time," I suggested.

"How's your car been running on the whole?" he asked.

"Great. Like the *Six-Million Dollar Man*, it's almost better than before."

"Fan-tastic!" He was happy for me.

I hoped he felt comfortable in my car. "How was the ride for you tonight?" I pumped.

"Fine. Just fine." He closed his eyes and asked,

"Where are the girls tonight?"

"They are with their dad."

"Do you have to pick them up?"

"Yes," I explained, "tomorrow is a school day."

"Have you thought anymore about private school? You know the Lutherans run a good program."

"I don't know," I said. "I need more time to think about it, and a miracle so I can afford it."

"Keep the faith. Pray. God will help you," he ministered to me and offered the kind of help I needed: gentle, kind interest in my life. He added, "Would you like me to come with you to pick up the girls? I'd like to help."

"You already have, Chaplain." I smiled my thank you to him. "I'm richer tonight just for this experience. I got a bottle of wine too!"

We drove back to the 'Downs in thoughtful-spot silence. It was getting late and we both were beat. When we made it through the security gate the Chaplain said, "This was a fine evening. We'll have to have more of these."

"Indeed," I said. We pulled up in front of his porch in better position for drop-off at his front door.

"I've got another box for you inside," he said, motioning me to come in. I followed. He opened the ever-unlocked screen door and pointed to a tattered box on the old gold living room chair.

I took the papered weight in my arms, "I'll be right back." I angled for the car. A flickering yellow porch light painted shadows across the open box top. Words of wisdom jumped off the scattered pages he'd gathered for me. SERVICE, CHAPLAIN, LEGACY and D-DAY flashed in a frenzy before me. A church service bulletin unfolded, falling open to subliminally advertise a good idea.

I plunked the box of papers in the boot of the car and hurried back up the steps to say, "Goodnight," and give him a hug. "Thanks again," we spoke at the same time.

"O Chaplain, my Chaplain, get some rest."

"Alright, Dear, you be careful going home. Be sure to tell those little girls their Chaplain says, *hello*, and all like that."

All like that echoed in my ears. It sounded like good news to me, in service to joyful memory. I picked up the girls from their dad's that night. When we got home and turned out the lights, I tucked them in. We all slept tight. Chaplain Barber's book became my silver lining dream's delight.

In this dream Grandpa Ted dropped by to show me another poet. It was Walt Whitman, wouldn't you know it? Walt and I walked for miles across rolling hills in lush green leaves of grass. He wanted me to stop lip-syncing, "*Don't be afraid to say or sing,*" he said, "*Become the Chaplain's poem.*"

"O Grandpa! My Grandpa!" I declared, "*My country 'tis of thee. Thank you for your poetry in three-part harmony.*" Warm at sunrise with eyes wide awake, my singing even breathing, I rose to record subconsciously in my morning pages this book's title into being.

VII

GOD MAKES SENSE

"We all have consciousness, and in that we have a feeling there is something out there, a spiritual force. This leads us to investigate God."

—Chaplain Barber, September 18, 2001

On the first Tuesday night after the saddest day in America I witnessed Chaplain Barber ordain his entire audience. I was there among them, seated alongside the mystified. There were boy scouts and military reservists, mothers, fathers, aunts and uncles, people from all walks gathered at the City of Commerce for a candlelight vigil.

The Chaplain had been invited to give the invocation. He used his five minutes well when he segued from prayer into superpower endower, freeze-framing us into an official new life of service. "Horses...D-Day...ice-cream...Amen...and guess what? You are all, hereby, ordained ministers! How about that?"

I glanced around the awestruck room. My eyes looked right, panned left and back to the right again. Quickly I reaffixed my gaze upon the Chaplain. Someone behind me whispered, "Can he do that?" Someone further ahead suggested he could, "I suppose so. Why not?"

Chaplain Barber cleared his throat and raised his hands to hush the whisperers. "There's nothing to worry about. Keep it simple now. Let's help one another. Love one another."

An enormous smile spread across his face to reveal the *Great Leslie*-esque gleam in his teeth. He beamed in God's delight. I caught the bright flash of his eye-sparkle as he made his closing remarks. "Just go out there and get the job done!"

God's newest ministers sat stunned in seven-second delay before the rousing round of applause. When we found ourselves on our feet for the ovation all judgment quickly faded. Our clapping became cheering which choked back the tears and confusion. We tried to catch our breaths, but we were swept out to the red, white and blue sea of American spirituality.

Moved. In the moment. Some standing next to me soared up, up, and away into the floating parade of flag-bearing boy scouts. They led the Chaplain across the aisles and out through the side door of the council chambers. He was granted safe, sacred passage. Like little sheep we followed, slowly flocking to where the night grew still outside.

There, "Amazing Grace" filled the air. Its melody played from a boom box on a bike. Many new ministers sang along. The crowd huddled close while I hummed. We passed white candles between our many trembling hands young and old. Some possessed praying hands. I saw hands-over-hands like pretty piano duets. Others held hands or did all they could to hold still. Together, ignited, we exchanged tiny flames for those we loved and lost. First, I remembered a *Lady Husker* named Julie. After the Bali bombing I would first remember Jake.

All one, a gathering aglow, we listened to the squeaking

cassette player rattle on to the next song by Lee Greenwood. I stared at the warmest candle nearest me which had begun to melt elongating ecclesiastical. Wax eloquent. I watched the white wax drip delicately down to the ground, mixing with hot tears fallen at my feet. The Chaplain's black shoes shined next to mine. In them I could see my reflection. My eyes, bewildered by the night, were burning bright in the light of candlewax white.

Why Me? I thought myself mute. *Me? A minister?* Me with my minister standing right beside me. He opened up my heart to all things possible come what may. *Is this the American way?* In a dizzying sway I became lost in the,"...*good old U.S.A.*"

*   *   *

Many full days later, during an afternoon drive back from the *Queen Mary* where we attended a Chaplaincy function, Chaplain Barber and I *talked and talked and talked* until my investigation of God made more sense to me.

CHAPLAIN: Ji-neel?

JANELLE: Yes, Chaplain?

CHAPLAIN: Did you enjoy today?

JANELLE: Yes, very much. It was especially nice to meet other chaplains and their wives.

CHAPLAIN: I'm anxious to read that book my friend gave you about his service as a chaplain during the Korean War.

JANELLE: Me too. I'll swap with you when I'm done.

CHAPLAIN: Okay.

JANELLE: What was it like to dine aboard the *Queen'* after all you experienced when she was the *Grey Ghost?*

CHAPLAIN: Oh, it brought back many memories. More important was having you there to take it all in. What about you? What thoughts raced through your mind when you stood in the old chapel there on the ship?

JANELLE: I role-played. I imagined myself one of your men, a soldier serving with you. Instantly, I was a Jewish serviceman standing in the crowded, makeshift chapel. A Temple to me. I watched the good cantor who helped you. I listened to you as you delivered God's message to me and my comrades in arms.

CHAPLAIN: How about that! Very imaginative.

JANELLE: It's important I learn to go where you're taking me.

CHAPLAIN: Do you do that frequently?

JANELLE: Go where you take me? Yes, literally and figuratively I guess you could say.

CHAPLAIN: I see. You remember the night when I ordained the crowd at the City of Commerce ceremony?

JANELLE: Like it was yesterday. Do you do that frequently?

CHAPLAIN: Ordain the masses? Oh, sometimes. When God in the moment calls. I find people can recover from their pain if they feel uplifted, when they feel they've been taken to new spiritual heights. This gives them a deeper experience. A chaplain's work is to help people with every facet of their lives as well as lead them to a closer walk with God. They need to know how important they are as individuals. Good individuals working together can change the world for good. Sometimes making them disciples, or part of the ministry, is important and I ordain.

JANELLE: Will making ministers out of a gathering in mourning lead them to a closer walk with God?

CHAPLAIN: I hope so. What do you think? I did that for you, too, dear.

JANELLE: You mean I'm <u>really</u> a minister?

CHAPLAIN: How about that? Congratulations!

JANELLE: So I'd better be careful what I say from now on.

CHAPLAIN: That's the truth. You just might be the closest thing to the Bible somebody ever gets to meet. Represent the Word well.

JANELLE: But I don't know my Bible as well as you.

CHAPLAIN: Don't you worry. God takes care of all that. You will know it. *To the Jews who had believed him, Jesus said, "If you hold to my teaching, you are really my disciples. Then you will know the truth, and the truth will set you free."*

JANELLE: Does being a minister really make that much of a difference?

CHAPLAIN: The only thing different is you know you're a minister. You can't baptize or marry anybody, but you can certainly go out and minister to others, hold their hands and bring them closer to God. There is simply more possibility, now and in the future, for you to make a difference.

JANELLE: My favorite word in all the English language is *possibility*. Isn't it possible you don't have to be a minister or a chaplain or take some special class in order to be of service to others? You simply have to open your heart to possibility?

CHAPLAIN: Now you're getting it.

JANELLE: But that takes away from your accomplishments doesn't it?

CHAPLAIN: Certainly not. Seeing people see the light only adds to my life.

JANELLE: What do you mean?

CHAPLAIN: God makes sense, Ji-neel. That's what I mean. No matter what happens in this world of ours, God makes sense of it.

JANELLE: How can you say that when people use God to wage wars and assaults against humanity?

CHAPLAIN: Look inside what you just said. People use God. They tend to twist things around and try to make God-sense out of their own nonsense. This does not work. God does not engage in assaults against humanity. Uninformed and unenlightened men do that. Don't become confused or spun into other people's confusion.

JANELLE: I have noticed how some people are quick to blame God when things go wrong.

CHAPLAIN: And how many people are quick to thank

God when things go right?

JANELLE: But that creates an imbalance to me. I think I'm growing more confused than before. Tell me more specifically how God makes sense to you.

CHAPLAIN: It's simple common sense. Jesus Christ was sent by God to show us how simple it can be to live together and love one another. It was people who ultimately grew confused. Christ's life was about love and peace and teaching and preaching and giving. We need to emulate that. It's that simple.

JANELLE: Be like Christ?

CHAPLAIN: We are like Him, even in each our own suffering. He went to the greatest of lengths and suffered for us. He paid the supreme price and sacrificed His life and died on the cross for us. And He was resurrected. This is our path to God as well.

JANELLE: Dying on a cross?

CHAPLAIN: We each have our own cross to bear. With Christ dying on the cross and resurrecting He showed us the way. God gave us our place here, this life, and He gave us Christ so we might have a hereafter.

JANELLE: So you're saying each of us lives a parallel life like Christ. He suffered, and so do we. He taught and loved and so must we. He gave and spoke, and so must we.

CHAPLAIN: Exactly.

JANELLE: Inside each of us He lives now, if we only let

Him. Through Him, we can know God, if we want to.

CHAPLAIN: That makes sense to me. You sound just like a minister!

JANELLE: It still all boils down to *experience*.

CHAPLAIN: Yes it does. Our given lives are our *experience*. And how we use our free will. God gave us freedom to choose no matter where we are. Here in America, our founding fathers emulated that with the notion that our nation would stick together and choose wisely. I don't think they had in mind how far out of line we would get. There's no excuse for poor decisions. No matter what our situation, we should make the right choices. I simply suggest we use God sense, choose in the like manner Christ would choose. That's common sense to me.

JANELLE: I've seen that catch-phrase at some of the churches we've visited, *What Would Jesus Do?*

CHAPLAIN: That's a good question.

JANELLE: God with an extra 'O' inside?

CHAPLAIN: Right. Yeah, right.

JANELLE: What if we fail to choose the right?

CHAPLAIN: We'd better recognize that error and never make it again. Repent and don't repeat mistakes. God forgives us when we are sincere in our repentance, when we are sincere in what we are asking of Him. He knows what's in our hearts at all times.

JANELLE: This is clear to me now, but how do I explain, or minister to someone who suffers from disease? How do I share with someone who has lossed a loved one? What about all the people who have died at the hands of others? I know what my grandfather endured. There is evil in this world. Why does God allow things like this to happen to people?

CHAPLAIN: I've been asked that before. First let me say that God has nothing to do with evil. God is only good. All good. All love. God created us. He loves us. He gave us life. Now the truth about life on this planet is it includes death. Death comes for every one of us eventually. But God loves us so much He gave us His beloved Son. Talk about pain and suffering? Look how young Jesus was when He died on that cross. Don't you think God was sad about that? And Mary? And everybody who loved and cared about Him?

Sometimes death fills us with sorrow. We feel sorrow when we care. That's because we have given to love. Love is what Jesus taught. Love and service. Our love and caring is what connects us back to God. And the good news is because God gave us His only begotten Son, death is not the end. Sorrow is not forever. Although each one of us must die of something one day, through Christ we will have an eternal hereafter where we can all be together again, free from any illness, pain, sorrow, suffering or affliction.

JANELLE: But that's only a guarantee if you believe.

CHAPLAIN: What's not to believe?

JANELLE: When my grandfather was diagnosed with his

cancer and given his allotted time left to live, we all sat around in disbelief.

CHAPLAIN: Cancer can be shocking like that.

JANELLE: After the passing of the news and the tears that followed, he summed it up by saying, "Well, I guess I have to die of something!"

CHAPLAIN: He's right. It's so sad, and I'm sorry you had to go through that with him, but he is right. It sounds like your grandfather understood this as his own God making sense to him.

JANELLE: After he articulated his personal understanding of his disease I began to question. I don't think I believed him or the doctors. I mean, how can they say, "Five months, five weeks, five days," when they are merely men who, according to God, *knoweth no hour*, right? Learning to stomach my grandfather's cancer caused me to reinvent my own belief system.

CHAPLAIN: Lessons can take a long time, and for some a lifetime. Your grandfather was how old when he passed on?

JANELLE: Eighty-nine years.

CHAPLAIN: That's a healthy lifetime. I know you loved him and he loved you. But God chose you to be with him when he passed on to Heaven. Be glad about that, Ji-neel. That was a God lesson, see. And I've got mine too. I've had to deal with death all my life. I can't even count the number of funerals. You know I had major bypass surgery too. 1981. God has shown me the face of death in many different ways, for His own reasons, and I trust Him and I will continue to put my faith and trust in Him. When Helen died from Alzheimer's in 1979, it was terrible. In a way it became my disease, too, because I didn't handle it well. I made some decisions I thought were right, but they weren't popular with everybody else. That's one of my crosses to bear.

JANELLE: Alzheimer's. It's taking so many good people right now. President Reagan. Charlton Heston.

CHAPLAIN: Helen didn't know who I was anymore and all like that. Alzheimer's. What a terrible disease.

JANELLE: Which is worse, disease or regret over how we respond?

CHAPLAIN: What a question. You know, we could spend a whole lifetime pondering our choices, mulling over our mistakes, wishing our lives had gone a different direction. We could try to escape our internal prisons by judging others or abusing ourselves.

JANELLE: Some people do just that.

CHAPLAIN: It's tempting. But we must not falter. We must remember our God-given life is not meant for that. We need to reserve judgment for God. He is the Judge. That's His job. Our job is to choose the right and through our acts of kindness shall we grow and encourage others to do the same. We need to do that lovingly not manipulatively or menacingly. Our job as ministers, as chaplains, is to invite people to hear the word of God, to understand the sense He makes when He offers His grace and forgiveness. And that's free for the asking. Ask away.

JANELLE: What if there are no mistakes? What if God knows what we are going to do and He lets us do it as part of our *free will* gift? What if part of our lesson is learning to use our free will to call on Him, to ask Him for forgiveness?

CHAPLAIN: What if you're right?

JANELLE: Then many people might need clarification.

CHAPLAIN: Another reason a chaplain's work is never done. Why are we here? Why did you and I meet?

JANELLE: You know, Chaplain Barber, that brings me to the question I've been wanting to ask you since we met.

CHAPLAIN: What's that?

JANELLE: You said chaplains never really retire. I can attest to the fact that you keep very busy. But everywhere we go together, even if it's just over to *Jack's*, you're wearing your Air Force uniform. Why do you do that?

CHAPLAIN: If I don't then people won't notice me.

JANELLE: Why is it important that people notice you?

CHAPLAIN: I don't meet a stranger. If I don't tell them about my story or give them my card, they don't get to know me.

JANELLE: Why do you think people need to know you?

CHAPLAIN: Because everyone I meet is one of the many who might need help. My uniform with this little lapel cross on it is a story, an open book, an open invitation to that closer walk with God. The uniform can speak louder than I can at times. If people hear it calling, I can slip them a card or a

Bible.

JANELLE: I see. And if the disciples didn't say anything...

CHAPLAIN: Exactly. We all have consciousness and that deep down feeling there's a God.

JANELLE: Is that the seed in every one of us that needs nourishment?

CHAPLAIN: Millions need nourishment. Many more don't know they need it. Some need reminding. Bottom line is, we all need God. There are no atheists in foxholes. *When there is nothing left but God, we find God is all we need.* We are all fighting our own battles. What better armor is there than the *Armor of God?* Christ's message. We all need food, water, shelter, love. My job is to share what I know with everyone I meet.

I engage people in conversation so they don't miss an opportunity and I don't miss one either. When God opens doors you need to go through them. In a way the cross is my uniform. I wear it as a preacher and I wear it as a chaplain.

JANELLE: What I'm hearing you say is our paths crossed because of the cross.

CHAPLAIN: In God's plan.

JANELLE: Tell me how the cross has helped you recover from your past.

CHAPLAIN: The cross is good at any time, past, present or future. God has always made sense to me and the cross of Jesus is the symbolic answer to all my troubles. I know I've made mistakes or made wrong turns. Sometimes I've been too trusting of people I didn't know were out to take advantage of me. Always, I would go back to the beginning and look for the truth at the cross. The truth can set you free, see. Even though we stray and break the rules and commit some sin, we can always go back to the cross and be forgiven.

JANELLE: Don't you think people take advantage of this or use this as a cover up?

CHAPLAIN: Only the confused. Remember what I said before? There is no deceiving God.

JANELLE: Can you be more specific about how forgiveness works?

CHAPLAIN: After you are baptized, the blood of Christ still covers your sin. You do this through prayer and through communion. That again gives the cleansing power of Christ. You again are cleansed and that can happen day by day if you live a life of prayer and service to God.

All the people that lived before Christ to Adam and Eve and down through all the prophets, they all sinned too, but they had great faith in God and wrote the scriptures for us. Their sins were all forwarded to the cross. As we've committed sins, those of us since Christ, our sins roll back to the cross. We can get to Him through faith and obedience to Him. Christ on the cross died for our sins. The cross is the center of history you see. Sometimes people need help in order to understand this.

JANELLE: Did you baptize men during the war?

CHAPLAIN: I've baptized people everywhere. During the

war in Europe I could be seen baptizing in the river, in the ocean. Chaplains have to baptize wherever they go.

JANELLE: So if I am called a sinner and if I believe in the story of Christ's life and death, and I follow His life of experience, if I believe, I get baptized and I am saved.

CHAPLAIN: Right.

JANELLE: But what about all the good people who aren't Christians? What about Buddhists and Hindus and so many others.

CHAPLAIN: God loves everybody and so should we. I love everybody.

JANELLE: What Jesus would do.

CHAPLAIN: First step is always love. Next, we as ministers of the Word must share what we know. The rest is up to God and free will. Of course, as God loves goodness we must strive to be good. As God gave us free will, we must use it wisely so others might follow our good example.

JANELLE: Be good because God is good.

CHAPLAIN: Common sense to me.

JANELLE: What about grace?

CHAPLAIN: We are saved by His grace. Everything we have is by the grace of God. Even our President has walked this road. Several years ago, he walked along the shores of the Atlantic Ocean in Maine, with Billy Graham. Billy ministered to him and he gave his life to Christ right then and there. I've worked with Billy Graham for more than fifty years. Through his great crusades I've seen him lead hundreds, thousands to Christ. His faith brought our President to finding his faith.

JANELLE: Leading by example. Can you give me more examples?

CHAPLAIN: On another occasion, we linked into Puerto Rico via satellite. Over a hundred and sixty thousand people were gathered sitting all around. I was there with Billy. He represented the Word of God and moved so many to Christ. It was 1967.

JANELLE: That's the year I was born.

CHAPLAIN: That means you've got hundreds, thousands of brothers and sisters. So many others were born again that year. It's so easy to give your life to Christ. Love Him. Love one another. Doesn't that make sense? I see only good in that.

JANELLE: You often refer to Billy Graham as the model for good ministry and spiritual leadership, a role model for your work as well. Tell me how you first met Billy Graham.

CHAPLAIN: I met Billy in 1949 in a tent meeting in Los Angeles and I've been walking with him ever since. Thousands had come to hear him. He was known to be a good preacher, an outstanding speaker. He began to take a hold of the hearts of prominent people. Even some shady characters were moved by his preaching. He baptized them. He baptized many people. Prominent people. Members of the Hearst family. For nearly eight weeks, that meeting went on.

I was pastor of the Park Avenue Church in Montebello at the time and would meet with him on the platform. This meeting went national and influenced a great many people and many church leaders. Ministers, leaders, laymen all over Los Angeles assessed the meeting afterward. Billy Graham became known as the national messenger of God for so many of us. The Little Brown Church in Hollywood was influenced. I've been there and worked with them lots of times too. That's where the Reagans were married!

JANELLE: What separated Billy Graham from the rest of the evangelists?

CHAPLAIN: Most evangelists would come to town and hold a meeting and take up a collection. They'd take the money and disappear. Billy was never about that. He said he was not going to do that. He said, "I'm going on a salary," and everything else went to charity or wherever it was needed. His purse was never padded. He remained steadfast and true and Christ-centered.

JANELLE: I appreciate that, but I never understood how a preacher could collect any money at all for himself, let alone go on a salary. Jesus didn't get paid and He is the Master Teacher! Who decides what a preacher's salary ought to be?

CHAPLAIN: That's a preacher's choice. Some denominations do things differently. Churches and their leaders and members have to make money because they have so much work to do to help others. There's nothing wrong with earning money. God knows we all need it.

JANELLE: I learned that the leaders of the Mormon Church don't take any money. They all earn their own way doing layman's work.

CHAPLAIN: That's one way. But if all you do is preach the gospel, in this day and age, you've got to make money, and everybody who works hard deserves to make a living. Billy kept it simple. I respected him for that. He ministered the truth and spoke and wrote about it and taught people what he knew and felt. His life is his ministry, a service to others, a service to God. In this he still had to provide for his family. Billy Graham has always been of service and he preached the Bible straight. He led many great spiritual crusades. In his lifetime he has come face-to-face with over two billion people. He is still leading people to God through Christ. What a ministry and what a modern marvel of a role model for any young preacher to follow.

JANELLE: As a young leader of a church, how did you collect money?

CHAPLAIN: We had to be creative. We did lots of things. Some people thought we could just put a little box in the back of the church and just depend upon the people to put in their offerings. That can work, but we took to passing the offering plate. I'd give a talk on stewardship and tithing. I'd pull from the Scriptures. There was never any pressure. People gave what they could when they could. However practical. We had to give money to make money in order to help each other out. It's really a simple concept. All kinds of organizations use it because it works.

JANELLE: I know teachers who donate their sick days

in order to help out other teachers who need to take catastrophic leave.

CHAPLAIN: That's tithing, a common sense system.

JANELLE: Tell me how you provided for your family as a young preacher keeping it simple?

CHAPLAIN: I made a small living as a preacher and then I had my military pay, but when I came home after the Korean War, my boys were teenagers and preparing to go on to college soon. I knew I'd never be able to afford university for them on my wages, so I had to add to my repertoire and find a way to make more money. I got into financial planning, life insurance, real estate investment. I worked first hand with some of the smartest businessmen in the country. People like Charles Schwab. This also allowed me to give more. That's the good thing about making more, it gives you the power to give more. Help. Be of service. All these aspects combined say I'm not just your ordinary country patriot, you see, I get involved with all sorts of things, events, opportunities and happenings all over the country and the world. I did this by following Christ, His example, and the good leadership of smart, spiritual people.

JANELLE: You said you've attended many of Billy Graham's crusades. I remember attending one at Anaheim Stadium during my drumming days with my little Crossroads Christian rock quartet. It was 1985.

CHAPLAIN: How about that! I was there, too.

JANELLE: There we were crossing paths, and we didn't know it.

CHAPLAIN: Isn't life full of interesting surprises?

JANELLE: Can you think of anything particularly interesting that Billy Graham did for you personally?

CHAPLAIN: Everything he said I took personally. I took it to heart. But not long ago he sent me my copy of the *Prayer of Jabez*. Through Billy Graham's preaching, and my commitment to following Christ's teachings, I feel that God has enlarged my waters.

JANELLE: In your waters are many "movers and shakers" besides Billy Graham.

CHAPLAIN: Yes.

JANELLE: I've seen you give pocket-sized *New Testaments* to civic leaders, business leaders, government leaders, public speakers, people you know or people you've just met. Why do you do this?

CHAPLAIN: Like the cross, for some it's just a memento. For others, it's a kind reminder of the *good news*. It also goes back to my message about D-Day. Like Christ, they were men who paid the supreme price for our freedom.

JANELLE: Why do you give the *New Testament* and not the *Old Testament* or the entire *Bible*?

CHAPLAIN: I've worked with the people at Gideon's for over sixty years and that little *New Testament* is all you need. Of course the entire Book is important, but it's the positive Christ message I'm about. It was those little pocket Bibles I gave out on that Sunday before D-Day that provided men with something positive, something hopeful. Good news. The *Old Testament* contains ten *don't-do-this-es* and *don't-do-thats*, whereas the *New Testament* tells us what we <u>can</u> do that's right. *Love the Lord your God* with all your heart and soul, mind and spirit. *Love your neighbor* as yourself. If you love like this you can't break a commandment. Now doesn't that make sense?

JANELLE: I think I get the picture.

CHAPLAIN: I think you do, too. It's a big picture but it's simple. It's service to God by serving others. Like Father like Son, another example is Billy Graham's son, Franklin Graham, doing his great work through Samaritan's Purse. Last Christmas over four million Christmas boxes were delivered to children all over the world. These boxes contained the only present those children may have ever received.

JANELLE: It's evident you like working with organizations who sponsor or care for children. When did this become an important part of your life?

CHAPLAIN: I've learned that every little act of kindness counts. They all add up you see. It takes kind adults to show a child how this works. Leading by good example. Ever since I was a little child I knew it took caring adults to help a child find his or her way.

JANELLE: How did you keep this ideology alive in your work as you grew older?

CHAPLAIN: I can tell you about some great work that was done during the Korean War. I was an Air Force chaplain stationed in Japan during that war. I was on the base in Honshu. Here's a little aside you and your dad might find interesting. The former Mayor of Atlanta, from Marietta, Georgia, was the commander of a unit stationed there in Honshu. He was the Colonel and a flier and a great Presbyterian believer. He was a churchman and he loved to play the organ. He'd come to the chapel and set up that organ and play by the hour. That just made things feel good like *Old Home Week* or *Family Night*. It's simple, maybe even trivial, but this little musical act was one way for a caring adult to show he cared about the people he was leading.

JANELLE: Was your family with you in Japan?

CHAPLAIN: My family was with me for a while. We had a little dog there too.

JANELLE: What kind of dog?

CHAPLAIN: I called him a Heinz 57 because he was all mixed up. Everybody else called him "Tipsy". It wasn't practical for a preacher's dog to be called "Tipsy" so when we brought him home we changed it to "Tippy". He was a cute little friend the children loved.

JANELLE: Dogs make great friends.

CHAPLAIN: They're so loyal. Do you have dogs?

JANELLE: My girls and I adopted two Collies from a rescue organization.

CHAPLAIN: Good for you. And good for them too.

JANELLE: They are very good dogs. Playful and protective.

CHAPLAIN: That reminds me of a little dog story I once heard. Did you ever hear about that mongrel dog of the Civil War?

JANELLE: Oh, yes! Grace at Gettysburg.

CHAPLAIN: How does that go again?

JANELLE: My mom and I took the girls on a car tour of Gettysburg not long ago. Our tour guide, a retired school teacher, fine-tuned the history lesson to meet our specific interests which were stories about women in the war, horses, and dogs. He shared with us a story about a stray dog who, on the days before the battle at Culp's Hill, had attached herself to the First Maryland division of Confederate soldiers. They named her Grace. When the Confederates were getting hit hard, Grace would stay with the men, licking their hands and cuddling them when they fell. She barked at the sharp shooters who eventually hit her, wounding her, but she kept on licking.

Regrettably, Grace was killed in battle on July 3rd. After the hill grew quiet and the Union soldiers moved in to survey their victory, their commanding officer said to his men that the only living creature who offered up Christian love on that hill, the only one who cared for others and offered service to others was this dog. He said, "Bury the dog first!"

CHAPLAIN: Grace. That's the one. That dog was the only one doing the Christian thing.

JANELLE: Caring for others in times of need.

CHAPLAIN: Service. That's the work I'm talking about.

JANELLE: Yeah, but look where it got her. Dead and buried and put on a monument.

CHAPLAIN: No, no. Never look at service for an outcome. Service is a selfless act done out of love and kindness. Sometimes duty. But all creatures great and small who perform acts of kindness are rewarded for it eventually. No matter what happens to them in life, all are rewarded for their service with the gift of Heaven. That dog is probably so happy right now licking the palms of every one of her soldiers 'gone onto Heaven.

JANELLE: So animals get to go to Heaven too?

CHAPLAIN: God created them. Why not? Everything God created will be part of Heaven too. All good things.

JANELLE: Did any other good things happen during your Korean War experience.

CHAPLAIN: I had a friend over in Korea during the war. Bob Pierce. He was over there as a war correspondent with Youth for Christ. He called me one day and said, "Russ, there are a hundred thousand orphans on the streets of Seoul, Korea." We decided to do something about it. We contacted everyone we knew. We got together and began to rescue those children. Out of that grew World Vision, one of the largest charitable organizations in the world. Out of that first group of children a little choir was formed. The little rescued children toured all over America singing. 56,000 Korean children eventually came to America after being adopted by American families. The Holt family in Seattle was a central part of this project. Last time I heard, Mrs. Holt, at age 92, was still active, running marathons, and serving God while serving the little children. A long life of service, that's reward. Through great Christian humanitarian service, over two hundred thousand children have been rescued worldwide. How wonderful is that?

JANELLE: Have you kept in touch with any of the children you came across?

CHAPLAIN: Sure. Some of the adopted children who grew up here wanted to go back to South Korea to see where they were born. I helped them make the right contacts so they could eventually get in touch with the President of South Korea. Many of them were able to return to their native land and visit.

JANELLE: Is it important that these children know that it was a Christian organization who helped them?

CHAPLAIN: We, as Christians, want to save every child of the world so they can grow up to know peace and freedom. Somehow, through this work I think they see the face of Jesus and they get the message that He loves them.

JANELLE: Is it important that they know it's Jesus?

CHAPLAIN: To me it is. And Jesus wants everybody to be saved too. I think it's love that matters first and foremost. Pure love. Once people understand love they begin to know Jesus, then they can grow in Jesus.

JANELLE: Do you have to be a Christian to do the Christian thing?

CHAPLAIN: You are a Christian when you do the Christian thing. There's nothing wrong in that.

JANELLE: That makes sense.

CHAPLAIN: Yes it does. The more you hang out with me the more you will see that God makes sense.

* * *

We stopped at *Jack's* after our good God talk. There on the bench outside the little corner cafe was a man about my age holding a Bible in one had and a wireless phone in the other. He saluted the Chaplain with his Bible side. The Chaplain approached him curiously, "Which scriptures are you studying?"

"I'm a theology student. I have a test tomorrow on Romans." His cell phone chimed the theme from *Exodus*.

Chaplain Barber looked at me, smiled wide, and bent over the theology student, "I know a little bit about that."

The man flipped open his phone. Like eavesdropping angels, Chaplain Barber and I quietly watched over him while he took his call. We heard the man acknowledge his need for a ride to the dealership which had finished repairing his car. Without blinking or thinking twice Chaplain Barber offered himself the chaperone and me the chauffer. "We can take you wherever you need to go," he announced.

On the way to the local Chrysler body shop the Chaplain and I discussed scriptures and practical Christianity with the theology student in my backseat. I mainly kept quiet with my hands on the wheel, listening while two like-minded men *talked and talked and talked* more Godsense into me. It was a gentle glide around the block, skimming over *Genesis* to *Revelation* with emphasis on *Romans* for the sake of the test.

"*While we were still sinners, Christ died for us,*" the Chaplain quizzed.

"*Romans 5:8,*" the student answered.

The two theologians were on fire with religious fervor for charity and the Word of God. Though I remained virtually silent, I could tell we were thankful we had met. "And never let us forget," the Chaplain said in response to the student's, "September 11th."

They expressed their matter-of-fact respect for church affiliates who had quickly raised and immediately gave millions of dollars to those directly affected by the fallout of 9/11. In my mind I pictured my two little girls photographed in black and white, dressed in oversized Fullerton firefighter suits with big fireproof boots on the day we donated their piggy banks at Edison Field in Anaheim.

"That's practical Christianity," they justified.

The young one leaned forward over the seatback and said to me, "Thank you so much for the ride. Now I'll be sure to make it on time to take my father for coffee."

I smiled when the Chaplain spoke for me, "No problem. We are here to serve. Now tell me, young Brother, what does your father do?"

The student leaned back. I saw him in my rearview mirror checking his watch. He patted the Bible resting on his backpack next to him. "My father is involved in housing for seniors," he said.

"Really?" Chaplain Barber sat up straight in his grey leather seat next to me. "Well, I'd like to meet him," he proposed.

Out of the corner of my driver's eye I could see the Chaplain's wheels spinning. He never missed an opportunity when it came to finding friends to network with. He leaned sideways toward me to dig deeper into his pants pocket. He said softly to me, "I'm going to give him my card."

The Chaplain held up his words-to-the-wise on white cardstock. "After you've passed your test, Brother, I'd like you to study my card," he professed. He swiftly shifted into a mini-version of his D-Day pocket *Bible* story. With emphasis he held up a Gideon's camouflage *New Testament* for the student to take home. The young man collected the card and the Book and braced himself for goodbye.

We pulled into Chrysler's drive. The sun was setting in the West. The Chaplain exchanged large sunglasses for his reading eyes. He laid out his plan for the student, "Let's you and I get together and talk about that senior housing."

I put my car in park and poised to shake the young man's hand. He looked at me through thick glasses. My vision penetrated through to his bright blue eyes. He had Chaplainy eyes. They sparkled when he said, "Thank you," and, "It was so nice to meet you both."

Chaplain Barber positioned his weathered hands into a silent prayer upon his lap. He paused, closed his eyes, drew in a deep breath and let go with a Fatherly farewell, "God bless you, Brother."

For a second or two, the theology student stood outside my car fiddling with the passenger safety lock. As he began to close his door he peered back in and said, "Chaplain, may God continue to bless you." The back passenger door closed. I cracked my window and shifted the gear into drive. Chaplain Barber sat quietly when I made my exit left. In the turn he became a silhouette framed by the blood orange backdrop of the setting sun. His shadowy presence spoke in an authoritative voice, "Good things happen everywhere when people work together. That's how God makes sense."

VIII

CROSSING PATHS

Praise God that good is everywhere; Praise
To the love we all may share, The life that thrills in
you and me; Praise to the
Truth that sets us free.

—Service Hymn #1,
Wings of Song Hymnal

ᎤᎵ ᎤᎵ ᎤᎵ ᎤᎵ ᎤᎵ ᎤᎵ ✝ ᎠᏂ ᎠᏂ ᎠᏂ ᎠᏂ ᎠᏂ ᎠᏂ

This is Chapter Eight. Swimming in a stream of consciousness, I meditate on eight. It is 8:00. An 8, sideways, is the infinity symbol. Infinity. Root word is "fine." Chaplain Barber says, "Fine!" all the time. In that context it means the equivalent of something very good to me. *Good is God with an extra 'O' in it.* An 8 is two 0's, one atop the other.

O, infinite 8! Isn't it great. 8 spinning is still 8. Crazy Eights. I played that game. A dollar sign looks like an 8 sometimes. Money comes and money goes, that's how it flows. Where it stops nobody knows. Put it where your mouth is and where it's needed most. A peanut is an 8. Sell peanuts. "Get your peanuts, here!" There are eight letters in baseball. B-A-S-E-B-A-L-L.

Didn't it begin in the 1800's? No-Peeky-Baseball, Grandma Frese's game.

A baseball game could have an infinite number of innings if teams remained tied. If the home team is winning, they only bat 8 times. Curve ball. If they are tied to what's right, tried and true, they are True Blue. Team players. I wore 18 on my uniform jersey. "Hey, One-Eight," the umpire called me to the plate. There is no 'I' in Team. 'I' is for infinite. Amer-I-can. Walt Whitman is an American poet whose work boldly asserts the worth of the individual and the oneness of all humanity. According to the American Heritage College dictionary, "infinite" and its synonyms- boundless, eternal, illimitable and sempiternal- amount to having no beginning or end. Serving humanity could be like that.

CHAPLAIN: Welcome to *Jack's*. I'm buying lunch today, Ji- neel. You order anything you want.

JANELLE: Oh, my goodness! I can't believe you own a wheelchair now.

CHAPLAIN: Puts a new spin on meals-on-wheels today. Have you tried those samples I gave you yet?

JANELLE: Oh, they were horrible. I don't know how you can stand to eat like that.

CHAPLAIN: Well, I try not to. But sometimes that's all there is. I'm grateful. Meals on Wheels is a very good service I will continue to promote.

JANELLE: You need to get out of that paper-piling dust bin, Chaplain, and into an assisted living center, don't you think?

CHAPLAIN: That costs an awful lot of money that I don't have. I have help. My doctor's got me all hooked up with a wheelchair and a walker. My son helps me. You help me. Everybody lends a hand. Everything is as it should be.

JANELLE: It just feels funny to me that you live alone and eat frozen meals after all you've done in service to others. How many years have you served in the Christian ministry?

CHAPLAIN: I've been of service to people all my life. If you count the years since my first sermon when I was seventeen, that's over seventy years. I still preach the gospel. I live the gospel. I love it. That's how I can say I'm never alone. God is with me wherever I am. I've got my telephone too!

JANELLE: And we all know you use it!

CHAPLAIN: I stay in touch with people all over the world. I have to. I got myself involved in so many things and it's my duty to make sure everything's working right. I share with everybody my experiences. They keep me informed of theirs. So many lives have crossed paths with mine. I don't know how, but they just keep crossing. Paths crossing paths through life. It's God's infinite power at work.

JANELLE: You said you remember having *an experience*, a spiritual awakening so-to-speak, when you were quite young. This led to your becoming passionate about spreading the gospel.

CHAPLAIN: That's right. I was Godstruck early on and it kept developing and growing brighter and brighter over the years.

JANELLE: You also mentioned the importance of having opportunities to develop your character, programs and camps that further influenced the well-being of your whole person.

CHAPLAIN: Yes. I attended camp, a Christian program, and ROTC in school. My mother made sure I got where I needed to be.

JANELLE: In your youth, in your development, were there any other influences you can credit for your life of service?

CHAPLAIN: One thing I'd like to mention is that the local businesses, businessmen, Rotary or Masons, they would take an interest in young people and help them to stay in school.

JANELLE: My grandfather led his Kiwanis Club in Huntington Park for years. In high schools, students today can join Key Club and work with Kiwanians in any city, business leaders and community organizations for good causes.

CHAPLAIN: That's good work. Organizations like this are what I'm about. When I was a boy these businessmen would buy a shirt or a pair of pants for a young boy or a dress for a young girl to make it possible for that young person to attend affairs of the city or to obtain a ticket to a ball park. On Wednesday afternoons, the whole town shut down to go to the ball park and see the Yankees at Avon Park in 1927-1928. That was a big event for people.

It always impressed me as a boy, the interest that a business-man would take in a young person to become involved, upright and honest. This gave us young people inspiration to think we'd have a chance in life too. The ultimate arm of that idea is Colin Powell's program *America's Promise: The Alliance for Youth*. This has challenged the whole nation to get behind our young people and give kids a chance. Little children are the future now. Mikayla and Marlena. Your pupils. Your little nephews. I know how I was influenced for the good as a young boy so I know from experience these things work.

The little red wagon is the symbol of that program. See, I wear it here on my uniform. I've been supporting this program for eight years, working with Colin Powell to capture hearts and make a difference in America and around the world. It captured my heart. Here, you take these little red wagon pins and give one to each of your girls.

JANELLE: Thank you. They will love these.

CHAPLAIN: Did you ever have a little red wagon?

JANELLE: I don't know if it was actually mine or not, but I remember playing with one when I was growing up. I filled it with little green army men and pulled it around the driveway. I think it was a *Radio Flyer*.

CHAPLAIN: What about the girls?

JANELLE: I couldn't find any *Radio Flyers* on the toy store shelves, but my mom and I were seduced by this Cadillac of red wagons at the Orange County Fair. We bought this glamorous thing that soars at twice the speed of sound while passengers ride in comfort with extra leg room and pillow-padded sides. It's more than just a wagon, it's Wonder-Wagon!

CHAPLAIN: I had a little red wagon too. It took me everywhere. I don't remember who bought it, but it was given to me at Christmas time. I hauled it around town. I remembered that wagon when Colin Powell came out with his program. Every little boy likes a little red wagon.

JANELLE: Girls too!

CHAPLAIN: Of course. That toy symbolizes so much. It especially represents the relationship between the child and the community family. One time I was wheeling around in my wagon a bunch of bags of fruits and vegetables and peanuts for sale. I was a thrifty little entrepreneur, see. I would pull that wagon until I sold everything. I'd take the money back to my mother and father so we could eat and make ends meet.

JANELLE: Tell me a story about those little red wagon days.

CHAPLAIN: While I was selling my goods door-to-door one afternoon, a nice lady came to her door. She called me by my name. "Well, hello, young Russ," she said, "what have you got there?" I told her what I was selling and she looked so concerned. It was getting cold outside and clouds were covering up the light. She noticed I didn't have a jacket and I might catch a frightful chill. She was so nice to me. She said, "You look cold," and she handed me her sweater right off her back. I said, "But how will I get this back to you?" She said, "Don't you worry about that. I'll see you in school next week and you can bring it to me then." She was my teacher! I hadn't even started school yet and she already knew my name.

JANELLE: That's service!

CHAPLAIN: Isn't it though? And what a small world.

JANELLE: In a small world more of us are bumping into each other every day. More than we plan for.

CHAPLAIN: Plan on it. When people meet life happens. And when that happens we need to be our best. We should always be prepared to meet people and greet people and treat people with kindness and respect. Just as we should be prepared to meet our Father in Heaven. There's a relationship there, an analogy for deeper understanding. Always be your best, do your best, and give of yourself. It's simple. Like the teacher with a sweater. I'm sure you are a teacher with a sweater too, Ji-neel.

JANELLE: I think I understand.

CHAPLAIN: What does this say to you?

JANELLE: It says I learn from every experience.

CHAPLAIN: Life learning your whole life long.

JANELLE: A student of any school, the school of life, chooses his teachers and should discern right from wrong. Teachers come in all forms but I look to higher consciousness. Not only is Christ the Savior, but Christ is the Master Teacher. As I live my life experience and I apply His teachings I become His student. As I grow in Him, I become a teacher too.

CHAPLAIN: Go on.

JANELLE: I am now recalling my fourth grade teacher, Mr. Horner.

CHAPLAIN: Tell me more.

JANELLE: He read to us and laughed with us and encouraged us to write our stories. As a lover of writing and storytelling early on, I was attracted to this style. It was what I needed at the time. Somehow in this experience I developed an affinity, not only for my fourth grade teacher, but for the role of teacher, for teaching in and of itself. In my fourth grade classroom I first felt truly accepted as a student and as a writer. I think this is where *experience* all began for me.

CHAPLAIN: And your teacher was just doing his job. It sounds like he was good at it too.

JANELLE: He was everybody's favorite teacher.

CHAPLAIN: Why do you suppose that was so?

JANELLE: Because he gave so much love and brought so much joy to his profession. Kids tuned into that. That's what I remember most about him. He made learning fun, even in competitive situations. I remember the race for the *Carl's Jr* lunch. Points were awarded for homework, test and project scores, and frequent displays of good character. The top three winners got a ride in Mr. Horner's cool car to the corner *Carl's Jr* for a *Famous Star*. He hooked us with his kindness and reeled us in to feel like winners. Everyone got a chance to win.

CHAPLAIN: That's what counts. Before what-plus-what-equals-what, we need to bring love and joy into the world. Your teacher did that and mine did too.

JANELLE: Altruistically.

CHAPLAIN: That's the key.

JANELLE: I've always thought, if there is love and kindness in the room, no child would be left behind.

CHAPLAIN: Good point. You certainly are one example of this ideology at work. Good teachers breed good teachers.

JANELLE: My father was a teacher too.

CHAPLAIN: How symbolic.

JANELLE: When he transferred from being a history teacher to taking on an administrative assignment his students surprised him with quite the farewell. They turned our house into a D-Day landing.

CHAPLAIN: Tell me about that.

JANELLE: I'll read it to you! I resurrected the article the other day because of its D-Day significance.

CHAPLAIN: Oh, do share it with me.

JANELLE: The student-driven stunt made the front page news in the local *Cypress-La Palma News Enterprise*, 1978. It was a living love letter to my dad, their favorite teacher. The headline reads: *Students' Farewell to Frese Is Spectacular. When La Palma's Mayor, Hank Frese, got home he found his yard and house had been transformed into D-Day.*

CHAPLAIN: Imagine that. Do you remember this?

JANELLE: Very well.

CHAPLAIN: Keep reading.

JANELLE: *The lawn and front of the house were covered with Marine Corps recruiting posters. The garage door held a huge sign proclaiming, "The Marines Have Landed," and flood lights came on to reveal the driveway had been converted into a landing beach. It was spread with sand and crawling with animated convoys of toy trucks and tanks pulled by nylon fishing lines stretched across the street where neighborhood operators crouched concealed behind parked cars. Hundreds of tiny toy soldiers marched everywhere. From the roof, at the first story level, girls were sailing paper airplanes made from camouflage paper. From the second story rooftops, toy parachutists with florescene-dyed parachutes floated down. The Marine Hymn blasted and battle noises poured from loud speakers. Cameras flashed and a movie camera rolled. From the bushes came sporadic "gunfire"* (firecrackers).

CHAPLAIN: Why did they choose the Marine Corps Hymn?

JANELLE: The students knew that my dad was also a lieutenant colonel in the Marine Corps Reserve.

CHAPLAIN: I see.

JANELLE: But he taught history and those kids remembered his lessons on World War II, D-Day in particular.

CHAPLAIN: This was well thought out.

JANELLE: Months in the planning. Eleven students and two teachers from Neff High School were in on it, plus my mom and brother and all us neighborhood youngsters.

CHAPLAIN: What was your role in the antics?

JANELLE: In the article it says, *Janelle Frese was in charge of interior designs.* I built a double column of tiny green men extending in through the front door, clear through the house, with one column heading upstairs and the other continuing out into the back yard where my marching men met their naval support, toy ships floating in the swimming pool.

All in all, *The allied forces deployed 2000 marines, 500 paper airplanes, 200 parachutes and rigged over 40 tanks and trucks as part of this spectacular going away present for a "really super teacher" Hank Frese.* I saved all those war toys too. I've got everything green, grey and plastic, from D-Day to the Guns of Navarone.

CHAPLAIN: Was your father surprised?

JANELLE: He was totally taken by surprise. He loved it. Here's the picture. You can see it in his face.

CHAPLAIN: Isn't that something? He's getting hugs too. I think the headline was right. Spectacular. This just goes to show what matters most. Good service. It's all in how we treat each other. Your father treated those kids so well and they loved him for it. They knew they were important to him, and he knew he was important to them. Just like you said that night on the phone.

JANELLE: My dad was the baseball coach too. One year his team baseball-carded the house. Instead of toilet paper they used baseball cards. My brother and I begged to clean up the mess later so we could collect the hundreds of 1960's and '70's baseball cards. We still have most of them. If they hadn't been hole-punched and strung up across the yard I bet they'd be worth a mint today.

CHAPLAIN: They are. You and your family enjoyed those experiences. Memories are our history, links to our past that teach us so much about who we are today.

JANELLE: What other links to your past can you make from this? What other experiences did you have? What else influenced you?

CHAPLAIN: How about selling my peanuts and candy and things at the ball park? You played 'ball. Tell me more stories about your youth!

JANELLE: I've spent lots of time in ball parks. I love the ball park. I sold lots of plain and peanut M & M's to support my teams. I grew up on the 'ball field. Girls' fastpitch softball. My dad was my first coach. You know your three P's- feeling the *presence, power,* and *peace* of God? My dad taught me the three C's- *confidence, courage* and *concentration.* I became a good player, both physically and mentally. I was eventually awarded a full scholarship to attend the major university of my choice.

CHAPLAIN: What would you attribute to your success?

JANELLE: I studied. I played hard. I prayed hard too.

CHAPLAIN: Which University did you choose?

JANELLE: UNL. The University of Nebraska in Lincoln. I played NCAA Division I Softball there for four years.

CHAPLAIN: Fantastic! What positions did you play?

JANELLE: I was a catcher my freshman year, then I switched to outfield.

CHAPLAIN: That's just wonderful. You saw the game from all angles. That's seeing and thinking outside the box! I bet you have a strong arm. Do you still play?

JANELLE: I played for a time in a professional women's baseball league. That was hardball, not softball. I used this strong arm to pitch.

CHAPLAIN: Right or left-handed?

JANELLE: Righty.

CHAPLAIN: I remember there was a woman a long time ago who could pitch so good she struck out Babe Ruth.

JANELLE: Jackie Mitchell.

CHAPLAIN: Who?

JANELLE: Jackie Mitchell. She struck out Lou Gehrig and Babe Ruth during an exhibition stunt. Lou was a good sport, but the Babe took it personally and made certain no woman was allowed to play in the Majors. I tell myself that's *okay* since women had leagues of their own anyway.

CHAPLAIN: When did you play in your professional league?

JANELLE: 1997-1998.

CHAPLAIN: You know about the Girls' league during the war and a bit thereafter?

JANELLE: Oh, yes. The AAGPBL. Some of their surviving members made guest appearances at a few of our games.

CHAPLAIN: You ladies probably had more fun than the men. Not much money was involved.

JANELLE: That could be true. I never thought about that.

CHAPLAIN: When big money gets involved people tend to do crazy things.

JANELLE: We all played for the love of the game while it lasted. We also felt that what we were doing was important. We saw women playing baseball at the professional level as a conscientious attempt to re-pioneer a place for girls so they might have the same kinds of hopes and dreams that little boys do. Dreams to make it in "the show" one day.

CHAPLAIN: There was an Air Force General, "Hap" Arnold, who was a pioneer for women's worth in the war effort. He supported Women Air force Service Pilots, the WASP's. He was a great leader and saw that women had an equally important role in making things happen. It takes visionaries like that to make all good things happen. I think it's great you have had the experience of pioneering something you believed in and you made a difference while doing it. Were you ever recognized for your efforts?

JANELLE: Not many people knew we existed, but after our inaugural season I was one of two pitchers given the first *Jackie Mitchell Award* for outstanding pitching. That meant a lot to me. I have that heavy black marble memory on my desk beneath your shrine.

CHAPLAIN: My what?

JANELLE: Your shrine. I have the outline for this book pinned up on corkboard mounted on my home office wall. There's a picture of you in your uniform, the recent one, and another from the laser copy of your horse cavalry days. I have a smattering of those Xeroxed articles and D-Day paraphernalia you gave me, and the 3 X 5 cards I'm using to get everything organized. I call it the, *"Shaplain's Shrine."* If my girls step into the office to see what's what I tell them, *"Sh! I'm shriting the Shaplain's book."*

CHAPLAIN: How about that. That's cute. Now tell me what the girls think about all this book talk?

JANELLE: They are very interested. Mikayla always asks me thought-provoking questions. The other day she said, "Mom, are you pleased with the book so far?"

CHAPLAIN: What did you tell her?

JANELLE: I said, "So far, so good, so God, and so it is."

CHAPLAIN: What about the little one?

JANELLE: Doing her best *Blues Brothers* impersonation, Marlena dons her dark sunglasses and says, "Excuse me, Mom, we're on a mission from God."

CHAPLAIN: I think she's right! Bless the little children. It's good they know what their mother is up to. Did your girls get to see you play ball too?

JANELLE: They were real little, but I have pictures of them wearing *Los Angeles Legend* rally caps, hanging out in the dugout snacking on peanuts. "Get your peanuts, he-ere!" My teammates taught them all kinds of baseball traditions, slang and superstitions.

CHAPLAIN: We have yet another thing in common. An amazing baseball connection. I sold boundless bags of peanuts at the ballpark. I always loved peanuts. When I was in Florida my mother would roast and boil peanuts in the shell, and after school I would sack those peanuts in small sacks and take them out to the ballpark. On Sunday afternoons we would all pile in my uncle's truck and drive thirty miles south to Avon Park to visit Gram and Gran Bowman. I saw Babe Ruth knock homeruns there when the New York Yankees came to train. I'd have my basket on my arm and my peanuts and such. Peanuts and candy I sold for 5 cents a bar or a bag.

We lived for a while in a place called Lake Wales, Florida. I'd sell peanuts on the street too. I developed quite a good business in peanuts and candy and fruit. After school, my other job was with my uncle who would bring the bundles of the *Tampa Daily Times* to all the towns. When he got to Lake Wales I took the papers from him and developed a paper route. I got other boys to work with me and we covered the town with papers. I was a successful entrepreneur. I was making $35 dollars a week as a boy. Of course, I gave most of it to my mother and father.

JANELLE: You've maintained a healthy work ethic all your life. What do you attribute it to?

CHAPLAIN: Positive guidance from caring adults. I was taught early on to participate in life, to take hold of every opportunity, to look for ways to make a difference. I think I made a lifestyle out of doing so. I still make connections with people.

JANELLE: Give me another living example.

CHAPLAIN: In 1948 a group of Christian ministers, myself included, and laymen too, secured ten acres of land that was donated up near Mount Wilson. This was donated land that was intended to be used as a boys camp. Later it was decided it would be for boys and girls with the Christian Church so kids could hear the gospel and further their personal development in Christ. We went up there, set up tents and began to dig. We built structures and set up a camp to serve a capacity crowd of about three hundred. Thousands and thousands have since attended Angeles Crest Christian Camp. I used to go up there during summers and speak to the kids. I spoke many times. I can even add a little romance to that! Talk about God leading people into crossing paths. Remember Larry Keene, the fine preacher you met when we attended Sunday services on my birthday last?

JANELLE: Yes.

CHAPLAIN: He met his wife, Virginia, up at camp. Virginia's father was one of the great founding fathers of Angeles Crest Christian Camp and I knew him quite well. When Virginia and Larry were teenagers attending the camp, they became good friends. When they grew older they started dating and they fell in love. They got married and together they have brought up one of the greatest churches in Southern California, that wonderful Church of the Valley.

JANELLE: Your life story is filled with thematic subplots of togetherness, partnerships with God making good things happen.

CHAPLAIN: You got that right. That's exactly what I am about. *With God all things are possible.*

JANELLE: In addition to Park Avenue, Angeles Crest, and the First Christian Church of Pico what other church organizations did you help build?

CHAPLAIN: The Whittier Drive-in Church. Before Bob Schuler's prototype, there was the Whittier Drive-in archetype! People drove in, parked their cars and hooked up the speakers to their car windows. Rain or shine they could hear the message of the Divine.

JANELLE: You held church services at a drive-in?

CHAPLAIN: We served donuts and coffee too. The manager of the drive-in had to open up for us. He obliged us and we held services from 1949 to 1963, nine to ten o'clock every Sunday. Thirteen years! I believe ours was the first ever drive-in church established. What a ministry! It was a shame it had to end.

JANELLE: Why did it fold?

CHAPLAIN: Like other organizations suffer, we fell under new management. A new manager came in who didn't want to open on Sunday mornings. The land eventually sold. Last time I drove by it was a weed-filled lot awaiting development.

JANELLE: Would you buy it today if you could and reopen the drive-in church?

CHAPLAIN: Oh, I sure would. We could hold Sunday services and during the week we could show family films. We could bring back little America to the big screen! We could donate our money to a good charity who needs it most. What a good idea.

JANELLE: You've said in so many ways that good ideas and life experiences intertwine. People meeting people in God-creative ways. We can attest to that. You and I have recognized our own patterns and connections, our two lives crossing paths again and again. Can you think of any other experiences that were, perhaps, foreshadowing for this kind of symbolism in your later years?

CHAPLAIN: I used to go with my mother to the city pool in Grant Park. There was a fountain there. People would toss in pennies and coins and things. I would dive into the water and collect as many coins as I could. I'd come up out of the water with all this copper in my mouth. A mouthful of money! I'd gather it all up and give it to my mother who I believed needed it most. I guess that would be symbolic for my life and how I have seized every opportunity, doing all in my power to make things happen to help somebody else.

IX

REVELATION

"Write, therefore, what you have seen,
what is now and what will take place later."

—Revelation 1:19

Water is emotion, and the day before all the changes took place I came home from an extended day's work to find my garden sprinklers still running since sunrise. The driveway was paved in swirling pot soil puddles. Taken by surprise, the girls and I soldiered over sidewalk seas and tip-toed across shallow waters to the safety of the front porch. I shut off the waterworks. Marlena spilled her bottle of water all over the entryway.

Once inside the house we turned to kitchen duties during which the dishwasher revolted in a foaming frenzy and the sink backed up in protest. We finally surrendered to finish homework and head early to bed. I found my old red NIV scriptures and read to the sound of rare California raindrops falling on rooftops. Godtears revisited. Thin paper pages turned to "Rock of Ages" in mental rhythm with my sleepy soul search.

In my dream the rain outside was knocking on my window. I saw clear water hands dripping wet, waving at me to wake up. Knee deep I made my way down the watery hallway. Water filled every room of my house. There were faucets dripping. The tub was overflowing. The kitchen sink spilled over like a waterfall to the floor. I closed my eyes and went under.

I followed the emotion channel from birth through my childhood to the power of now. I swam the current. Tense but not terrified I rode a tidal wave out the back door, out to sea. I held my breath and dove down into deep ocean blue looking for the truth of who and why I am. Lost in the stream of consciousness I resurfaced like a bobbing pocket Bible and floated downstream to Battleground, Washington, where I climbed out on the river's edge by Grandpa Ted's rapids. He grabbed my hand and guided me over slippery rocks to calmer water on the other side. With him by my side I searched for the fish of rainbows. We waded through waving clear water hands heading upstream to the quiet fishing cove where Uncle Irv waited with Lady, his collie dog. Chaplain Barber met us there. He was holding my life preserver. The voice in my dream heart said, "Jump in the water and take it." I must, "Trust the living water," to carry me safely back home.

After I awoke drenched in sweat from the night's cold soaking I bumbled down the corridor toward my home office. I walked through the door to record my dream. While riting my way through my morning writing, a robotic voice interrupted saying, *"You've got mail."* I checked to see there were nine new messages lying in wait for me. The bottom of the ninth selection hit me hard like a hammer to the gut. Wide awake awash. It ruined my day like torrential rain in a flood zone. Not until I prayed over it was I able to call the Chaplain hoping he could explain.

"Chaplain Barber," I began, "I received this mysterious e-mail from an unable-to-reply-to, anonymous sender. It bamboozled me, really knocked me off my marching feet."

"What did it say?"

"It wasn't very hopeful, Chaplain. It read, in effect, that you are just a nice old man, looking for some company and a free meal."

"That's not far off for any of us!"

"I'm serious. It went on to imply if I continue to write this story, I'm only wasting my time, running the risk of publishing far fetched fabrications."

"Oh, boy," he sighed.

I emphasized, "It sucked the wind right out of my sails. Now I'm treading water, dreading this call, doubting doing this writing. Can you help me out?"

"Who sent you this?"

"I don't know."

"All this wallop from a phantom?" He explained, "Let's sort this out together. Now, I can't think of who would want to suggest something negative about me, but I know who I am. I also know that no matter how much good we try to do, we will always have our adversaries. Christ had His adversaries too. *Love thine enemy. Forgive them, for they know not what they do.*"

"Bottom line, Chaplain, I need to be clear. Are you the man of service I believe in? Tell me, please, you are not another moth after the star?"

"What's that?"

Trying to breathe in the midst of creative blockage, my flow bleeding out from the stoppage, I was drowning. To save myself from being late to work I had to cut the Chaplain off. "I've really got to end this call, but can I come see you after school today?"

"Alright, Dear, but don't you worry now. Give this thing to

God," he said. I hung up the phone on, "God."

I went to work where this e-mail kept stored in my thought process was stewing in my creative juices all day. Later, when I met up with the Chaplain in his living room headquarters, I learned another lesson.

I arrived just before twilight and parked behind his non-operationed Oldsmobile. I couldn't remember the last time he had driven it. There was a new dent I didn't recognize. Intent on pounding out this email dent, I metaphored my beloved parable and began the inquisition.

"The Moth and the Star is a moral story by James Thurber," I said.

"Tell me how it goes. Let me have it," the Chaplain ordered.

I retold, "Well, there's this strapping young moth with his sights set not on any porch lights or street lamps on about his town. Rather, he's stuck stargazing on the twinkling star just above the tree tops. His mother and father think he's being ridiculous, too ambitious, and they suggest he go out and be like everybody else."

The Chaplain pinched his chapped lips with blue fingers from his bruise-battered hand. "How's that?"

I stared at his hand in narrative, "They wanted him to get his wings singed and such like his brothers and sisters had done. After they all burned to death at very young ages, this crazy moth lives on to a ripe old age still desperately trying to reach that star. He never does reach the star. He only makes it to the tops of the trees, but he gets so old and nobody he knew is around anymore to say otherwise, he starts believing he has actually reached the star. He eventually goes around saying so."

"Fan-tastic!" The Chaplain leaned back and beamed with delight. "That's a great story!"

I followed his hand to his knee. His relaxed candor surprised me. As if he missed my message I tried to justify the analogy. "It's one of my all time favorite stories, but it's got me worried because it reminds me of you."

"Oh, dear." He shook his head slowly from side to side and out from his lips puffed a breathy motorcycle-mumble. This was the start-stop sound he made only when he felt uncomfortable. He sat mute for a moment before scratching his chin.

Steadfast in a state of worried demand I struck back, "Well?" I fished for more from him. He fidgeted with his glasses. I tried cashing in on shock value, "I'm stuck, Chaplain. I can't write a DAMN THING!"

It paid off. "Hold on a minute!" he commanded. "Don't panic, Ji-neel." He leaned in closer to me. "You know, there are people all over the world with stories to tell and people all over the world who need to hear them. I know what I have to say is real and important. It happened. That's the truth. I was there. Now I ask you, why would my near ninety years cross paths with your thirty-six if it weren't part of a great true story?"

"For a good reason. I hope." I groped for resolution.

"Right," he said, "Hope. More importantly, faith. Through this friendship, Ji-neel, our fellowship in Christ, this book, haven't you come a little bit closer to understanding why we are here?"

"I have," I humbled.

"Is that a good thing? Is this God with an extra 'O' in it?" He found my heart string.

"It is," I cut him some slack, "but I need proof, Chaplain Barber," I grumbled still resisting.

"Have faith. Don't let a pest with nothing better to do infect your whole way of thinking. That's how people get confused. You probably got a whole bunch of good e-mails this morning and you chose to focus on that single aggravating one. You let the sniper have access to sneak his way in."

"You're right. I did," I confessed.

The Chaplain then voiced the foundation of my true being, "Focus on the positive, Ji-neel. Use your own *Power of Positive Thinking* and let God go to work in you. You know who I am. I KNOW you know who I am."

"So are you positively who you say you are? You have really done all these things?" I called in for reinforcement.

"Of course, I am. I am Colonel Chaplain George Russell Barber. I am a Christian preacher and a proud father, grandfather, great-grandfather, a chaplain, a man who still serves. I made the landing on Omaha Beach on D-Day. I have served from the horse cavalry days to the Space Age and right on through to this war on terrorism. I've walked and talked with great leaders and held the hands of the weak and weary and all those in between. I am history!"

The Chaplain was back in his pulpit, pontificating from the pedestal on which I once again placed him. In his, "history!" my head began to spin. Inside my soul, twisting, contorting, I began to speak in tongue-tied tongues. I said something like, "We are re-living in history."

"Right, Ji-neel. Living history. My life is no mystery. It's all right here. Ask me anything."

Riddled with guilt bullets I held myself in contempt, "Now I feel terrible."

"You know Bob Dole has a funny way of looking at things like this. He simply agrees with any nay-sayers before they nay-say. He says to them, goading them, *'My story gets better every time I tell it! The older I get,'* he says, *'the fewer people there are left behind to dispute the bettering of my story.'* I got a letter from him here. Would you read it to me?" The Chaplain handed me a Xeroxed copy of his letter from Bob Dole.

"Sure, Chaplain," I said. "He writes,

> *Dear Russell,*
>
> *It was wonderful to see you in July for the dedication of the Dole Institute in Lawrence. Your participation in the dedication ceremony still means a great deal to me, and I will always cherish the thoughtful, memorable words you delivered on that special day."*

"Isn't that nice?" Chaplain Barber added, "This should be part of my story too."

I finished reading Bob Dole's letter as the Chaplain nodded along.

> *"On another note, I would like to personally extend an invitation to you for the dedication of the World War II Memorial in Washington on Saturday, May 29. The Memorial dedication will honor the thousands of veterans who risked and sacrificed their lives in the name of freedom, honor and duty to country. On May 29, the entire country will pause to remember those of us physically present at the dedication, as well as those present in spirit. While our World War II greatest generation is significantly smaller in numbers than in 1944, the memory of our service to America will be forever preserved in the Memorial.*
>
> *"As the last surviving chaplain from Omaha Beach in Normandy, your service to America, to Americans, and to others around the world will never be forgotten. Know that your contribution lives on in the hearts and minds of many throughout the world. Consider this a truly personal 'thank you' from a fellow serviceman who*

deeply respects your honorable service and your contributions to humankind.

> *God Bless America,*
> *Bob Dole*

"Wow, what a letter, Chaplain."

"How about that, Ji-neel. Now if Bob Dole knows who I am don't you think you can rest assured on it that this book is worth your time? It's your story as much as it is mine. You can just delete that email."

"I feel like I've committed treason, Chaplain Barber. Isn't treason punishable by death?" I felt forgiven yet showered with shame. I tried to reason, but wrestled instead with the pain of questioning. "Everything happens for a reason, right?"

"More than our capacity to understand," the Chaplain explained. "You know there are so many of us in my generation walking off into the sunset each day. I know this next generation is just as worthy, but I worry sometimes there will be no one following after to stand up and represent what is true and what is just and what is right. In many ways I think I am counting on you to carry the message, to run with it like an Olympic torch."

"But how can I when I'm just a working woman without any military background?" I wallowed in unworth.

"You've had military background. What do you think this is? You've learned all about my life in the service. Your father served. Your brother serves. You showed me your picture all decked out in fatigues on that D-Day surprise at your house. Heck, we met at the eternal flame on Memorial Day. You can carry this torch. Remember what I told you about your writing when you doubted yourself?"

"Tell me again," I begged for his merciful pardon. "Remind me, please."

"God chose you. You've been hand-picked by God for this job. This is your calling."

"If my stomach is twisted in knots must I answer?"

"And persevere," he preached.

I heaved a heavy heart sigh and asked him, "Is my perseverance this torch you describe?"

"Think about all those young men who paid the supreme price on D-Day. Think about Christ who died on the cross. Now ask yourself that question again."

"I think I am overwhelmed. With writing this, only one of my duties, I must compel readers not just to read, but to believe, to go to work, to serve, to love one another like God loves us. How do I do that in the face of opposition? I never thought my life would have me doing what Jesus would do."

I couldn't believe what words escaped me. Just then, behind the Chaplain's head, I saw the fringed living room lamp timer-on to a golden glow. Light shined like a halo around the Chaplain's crown. This event, effervescent, made me thank God for him like never before.

"Don't you worry about any outcomes," he ministered to me. "That's God's job. You simply do the basics and He'll guide everything else. Go back to the beginning."

"I do that often." I said.

"That's good. Always go back to the basics. What compelled you to come shake my hand that crisp cool day?"

Taken back, "I was moved by your stories. And your Chaplainy charm. In a nutshell I was inspired by you."

"That is the key to life learning, the essence of *experience*.

Be inspired. That is wonderful. You are wonderful. I hope my life story, the things we've recorded in this book, can lead to someone gaining inspiration, faith, love, or all of the above. I like to think my life has been about service and I would like to leave behind that recipe. Let's give readers an *experience*. Now tell me, what will my book be called?"

"I thought about *Chaplain Barber's Pocket Bible*. What do you think?" I brainstormed with him.

"That's nice. Will people know what they are getting? Does it sound too religious?" he critiqued.

"I thought about calling it simply, *The Chaplain*."

"People might get that confused with a comedy or an actor. I enjoy a good laugh, but maybe there's another title in the bag for us."

"You said you'd like to leave behind the '*Recipe for Service*,' and that's a fitting metaphor for your life's work, all you've cooked up over these many years," I slowly stirred in more ingredients to the mix of titles.

He tried to visualize, "How would that look on a cover?"

"With service as your theme, how about *Service: A D-Day Chaplain's Legacy?*"

"Fine. That fits so far," he gave me a confident smile. "Can we fill it with our conversations?"

"And prayers," I added.

"And your meditations," he mix-mastered.

I sprinkled in seasoning, "With our personal dedications."

"I like how this is taking shape." He folded his arms and asked, "How long will it be? I don't want it to be too long."

"Chaplain, remember, you've got almost ninety years to cram into one book," I reminded.

"I know, but I want to keep it simple. Short and sweet and

straight to the point. I think readers would stay more interested that way."

"And your hook for your book?" I looked for more structural support.

Calmly, confidently, he concluded, "There might be a reason I have become the last living chaplain from the D-Day landing at Omaha Beach."

"O Chaplain, I'm so sorry I doubted you." I felt the tears building up, raising the water table inside me. Floodgates flexed to burst.

"Don't you go worrying about that. Everything's fine, as it should be." The Chaplain's tone took me to a vision of Tom Hanks who told us all, "*There's no crying in baseball.*"

I wished my tears away, but they had come to stay, my pitiful penance to pay. "You have a natural knack for bouncing me back, Chaplain Barber, to the business of forgiveness," I wiped my eyes temporarily dry to receive my official pardon.

"There is nothing to forgive. You are doing such a great job, and God and Christ are with you. *Let's pray…*"

During the prayer that followed, tears fell like parachute flowers forming soft puddles on the Berber floor. I fought back the private *How could you's?* that threatened to attack me again. That e-mail assault on my emotions pushed me over a new challenge course edge. My resolve was to kill that e-mail with kindness, forgiveness and downloads of information.

Later that week I countered with an internet tribute to Chaplain Barber, true friend and spiritual champion. After school one day I deployed two of my technologically savvy students to the front lines. There they confronted the computers lined up in my classroom. My students my teachers, they taught

me how to design a web page filled with facts detailing the story
of Chaplain Barber, man of service.

This tribute will remain fit, armed and loaded with
information anyone interested may access. It will be a good
example of the positive usage of technology. While the Carpenter
is still working on it, at any time you may visit:

www.livingdday.com

To thank me for the tribute the Chaplain invited me to attend
another event with him. Had he been well enough to go, it would
have been one like the annual Congressional Club meeting we
attended together in Orange County one year ago. On that
particular occasion we enjoyed our time at the philanthropic
House of Design, "a worthy cause," the Chaplain identified with.
He said we'd get to schmooze with, "the movers and the shakers,"
of our state and local government. There would be senators and
representatives, judges, philanthropists, other veterans, business
and community leaders to, "rub shoulders with."

There the reigning *Ms. America* led us in the *Pledge of
Allegiance* and our *National Anthem*. I spoke with her after she
sang. She asked about the Chaplain and this project, and she
shared with us a piece of her father's past that took us traipsing
back over the paths of the second World War. Her father was an
Army Air Corps flier who earned sixteen distinguished flying
crosses, all of which she found in a box he'd left behind for the
world and her to find.

Speaking to Ms. America about her father made me wonder
how many other personal histories lay dying in boxes under
beds or suffocating in storage trunks in piling system garages.
I quickly eyed the Chaplain with thoughts of preserving his

treasures wherever they may be. We *talked and talked and talked* about that on the taped drive back.

JANELLE: Chaplain, it would be ideal to add to this book some pictures and memorabilia, perhaps the letters you wrote to Helen. What do you think?

CHAPLAIN: I think that would be wonderful. There are two old trunkloads filled with those many wonderful, historical things. All my uniforms I wore over the years. My boots. That Bible that survived D-Day. My military papers. Pocket Bibles. Photographs and letters.

JANELLE: Helen's and yours?

CHAPLAIN: I wrote to Helen almost every day during the world war. Sometimes twice a day. She wrote to me and sent me pictures of the boys. I saved all that too.

JANELLE: What about your medals and citations. Which ones did you receive?

CHAPLAIN: I received all kinds of medals including the Bronze Star for my work in landing on D-Day. Everybody gets a little colorized bar for their work wherever they serve. I wear fourteen different bars on my uniform.

JANELLE: What about your paper, *The Limit to Toleration of Alienisms in America?* Is that stored too?

CHAPLAIN: That's somewhere in those trunks along with all sorts of documents, scrapbooks and ribbons and things.

JANELLE: These sound like treasure chests to me.

CHAPLAIN: They are.

JANELLE: Oh, this is so exciting. I feel like a kid in a candy store. When do I get to explore?

CHAPLAIN: You don't.

JANELLE: What! Why not?

CHAPLAIN: They're gone.

JANELLE: Gone?

CHAPLAIN: Lost.

JANELLE: Stolen? You've got to be kidding me?

CHAPLAIN: Nope, it's no joke. It's been about ten or fifteen years ago now. I had them stored in a garage. When I moved to the mobile home park somehow they vanished.

JANELLE: Oh, my God!

CHAPLAIN: Now don't go bringing God into it! He had nothing to do with it. Whoever took my things is solely responsible, not God.

JANELLE: I just can't believe a person could do that, take all your personal treasures away like that. This makes me sick.

CHAPLAIN: I know. It's very sad. These are things my family should have been able to keep for years and years.

JANELLE: You could have donated some things to the D-Day Memorial or to the Museum.

CHAPLAIN: Well, I guess we could share this book!

JANELLE: That's an idea, but it doesn't make me feel any better. Have you tried searching? Did you post any *LOST* signs or *REWARD*? Did you place an ad or public announcement? What about catching the thief on E-Bay?

CHAPLAIN: You know, Dear, sometimes terrible things happen. There is no ready rhyme or reason for any of it. Those are the times you have to let it go and give it to God. He's good at sorting these things out.

JANELLE: Come on, Chaplain, I'm sorry, but you have been violated. This is NOT okay and somebody needs to answer for it.

CHAPLAIN: He will in God's time, but please understand I've tried. I've looked around. I've asked. I hoped and I prayed. I thought those storage trunks would find their way back to me. I assumed, since my name is all over everything, some things might surface and be returned. Maybe I didn't have enough faith. In the back of my mind I always thought whoever has them knows they've got valuable treasure. The monetary value probably means more to that person than their conscience leads them to understand my sentiment.

JANELLE: So it boils down to money?

CHAPLAIN: Money, money, money.

JANELLE: Money is the root of all evil.

CHAPLAIN: I certainly think it can be. Money helps a lot of people though, too. Maybe my things have helped someone get by, but I understand what you are feeling. If money or reward gets rooted in someone's heart and soul, instead of

God gripping their heart, well, that can cause a person to do evil things.

JANELLE: Like steal your treasures. And besides the thief, who is the buyer? Why doesn't he step forward and up to the plate? Who are these people? What is wrong with them? My heart is just broken for you. I can't fathom the heartache you must have endured over this.

CHAPLAIN: Somebody had one heck of a garage sale.

JANELLE: *Somebody* ought to be ashamed of themselves. Is nothing sacred anymore?

CHAPLAIN: Things, Ji-neel. They are only things.

I meandered my way back home alone, longing for reasons, denying God's seasons. On this solitary drive I took surface streets, turning down curvy roads this way and that. It was a micro study of *Why Me?* I bobble-headed in the car, heading in a right direction as the setting sun reflected horror orange in my rearview mirror.

With one hand on the wheel and the other reaching back I found my black cd storage box. I blindly fished for something to ease my mind off insidious crime. I pulled out an old Tom Waits collection, something I had not listened to in years. I slid the disc into the slot and hit the *Random* button on the player.

"Soldiers Things" played first, an accident on purpose like lost treasure found. I made a wish for my mother to find Grandma Theone's ring, then sad song suffering swept over me. Grandma Theone never got to see me play. Her ring is among the missing along with Chaplain Barber's ornamental past. I wept the rest of the way home, driving 'round and 'round the tired towns.

In the twists and turns a familiar fog rolled in. Images of overstuffed storage trunks clouded my mind. My funny God-guides suddenly appeared. Wee frantic fairy muses wearing tiny medic helmets were pushing and pulling, *Heave! Ho! Ho!*-ing the Chaplain's good things down a dusty road to nowhere.

Written in their medical journals were tiny job descriptions that included the duty to put a smile back on my face, if only for a song. Their remedy was ready-made medicine for the melancholy. Muse-ical healing. They doctored me with silly sponges sopping up the tears that pealed back the years, layer after layer of me looking for meaning in life. Somewhere in the floating factory of notes I unearthed a new human capacity for understanding things. Things. Soldier's things. The somber song played on.

"SOLDIER'S THINGS"
By Tom Waits

Davenports and kettle drums
and swallow tail coats
table cloths and patent leather shoes
bathing suits and bowling balls
and clarinets and rings
and all this radio really needs is a fuse

> *a tinker, a tailor*
> *a soldier's things*
> *his rifle, his boots full of rocks*
> *and this one is for bravery*

and this one is for me
and everything's a dollar
in this box

Cuff links and hub caps
trophies and paperbacks
it's good transportation
but the brakes aren't so hot
neck ties and boxing gloves
this jackknife is rusted
you can pound that dent out
on the hood

a tinker, a tailor
a soldier's things
his rifle, his boots full of rocks
oh and this one is for bravery
and this one is for me
and everything's a dollar
in this box

My girls went with my parents for the weekend, giving me time to take everything in. My mind needed riting. Writing. Righting. Time to rethink, digress. To imagine. I imagined what my life might be like without things. I cursed the devilish systems of want and scoured the house for my own.

I rifled through my own hope chest that slept beneath my bed. It was filled with faded photographs and cracked paper memories, shiny satin sentiments and scattered remnants of my childhood dreams. So many little things took me back to distant lands where freedom songs played me to the levee and I marched along to the beat of my own sacred drum.

My beautiful grandmother in her wedding dress smiled at me black Swedely, Grandpa Ted standing tall beside her like he always did. That was then, and in the now, photo negative ghosts behind my back brought me all the way back into my painbody, wrought, distraught, rueful and restless. Pictures and things. Only things, things that can do so much.

A God message trickled down my cheek, teaching me we all must suffer from the pains of our past. Perhaps this is why we want. Maybe we are connected this way, strung together like baseball cards, paper-proud dolls falling away and into systems. I yearned for the Chaplain to explain to me sinning and the restoration.

When I called him that night, just checking in, he said I need not worry. "We're in good hands," he said. "You know our Congressman Ed Royce? He took good care of me. He retrieved over 700 pages documenting and detailing my career. It's all there. I've got it all up here in my head too, just like you've got it written down in your pages, Ji-neel."

His voice of reason was my practical Christianity, wised up in my soul. I thanked God for the touch of gold. "I've got it all right here in my heart next to you, Chaplain Barber." I stood tall like Grandpa Ted by his word. With God's *Word* and in His name we prayed for the last time over our phones from our homes.

By the end of 2003, the year of transformation, Chaplain Barber was finally convinced it was time to sell his mobile home and move to a place where somebody else could care for him. In the whirlwind of change giving in to time his health began to decline. His private stay in a plush assisted-living center was short-lived. He landed exhausted in the Presbyterian Intercommunity Hospital for dehydration observation, of course conversation, and eventually, an operation.

I avoided calling him. I avoided medicine as I was already weak with internalized terror. I wandered my hallways wondering who might answer his phone and what that person might say to me. The only thing that separated me from fear and opportunity was prayer.

I prayed like it was only up to God. I finally picked up the phone and dialed like it was only up to me. Working together, God and I shined bright, warm light through my old shadows to find the same old Chaplain Barber alive and kicking like Grace.

"Ji-neel!"

Thank God, "How are you, my Chaplain?"

"Operation over, under the Lord! Come and see me, my dear. You know where I am."

Only visitors twelve years of age and older were welcome at the hospital. In the circular drive I selected Valet and tipped the parking attendant. He let me sneak the girls through the main entrance. We made it to the check-in desk where I signed in, received a guest pass and secured the Chaplain's room number. Room 316. I thought of John.

The checkpoint security officer looked at me curiously and scanned over the girls. "And how old are they?" he asked.

"Twelve," I sinned.

The girls straightened tall and gave their widest and brightest smiles. They asked where the bathroom was located. Looking away from his desk, the uniformed informant pointed toward the lobby. We quickly maneuvered ourselves out of his sight. The three of us girls made a game out of learning the cold hard facts of hospital logistics. We read wall maps and solicited the alliance of sauntering, semi-retired security officers in our strategic sneak operations.

"We're on a mission from God," Marlena justified. On this trip, our first hospital visit, Marlena rode up the elevator accidentally by herself. "Mo-omm!"

Her voice faded out as she sent herself up to the third floor without us. Mikayla and I popped panicked glances at each other and watched the elevator lights go up, up and away, and gently back down again to reveal Marlena standing still, alone in the middle of the elevator, palms opened up to the mirrored sky inside.

"Oh-my-God, Marlena, pay attention!" Mikayla mothered her instead of me. I, on the other hand, hushed by the rush of guilt, had gone into the Otis cab to give Marlena a great big hug. I held her as she fought back her retreating tears.

We stuck together the rest of the way, ducking around corners and slinking side-by-side down silvery clean corridors, slipping through the lite-bright doorways that led to Room 316. John was in there. He was sharing a room with Paul-Something-Jr. They were divided by sliding ceiling curtains.

There was no George Russell. No Chaplain Barber. I stopped breathing. Silence monitored. Mikayla, my untwelve-year-old, muttered, "Hello?" to the resting roommates. She turned to me and whispered, "Mom, maybe we should go."

Loud and clear, Marlena announced our presence to everyone,

"We're on a mission from God." We paused to ponder, poised to run. After our brief moment of reflection we bolted invisible back down the sterile aisle.

A tiny grinning nurse in white cotton scrubs crossed our path. We blurred past her with a whirring undisturbing gust of hospital ghost between us. Using the eyes in the back of my head I watched as she followed us floating up and down the hall. We curved around the corner like a comet. The nurse nodding her head, sparkling in our dust trail, was an angel in a human suit. Only she could see us.

She called out, "Come ba-ack," which caught my attention. "Wait! Come back." We turned to look at her and froze in our footsteps. "Are you looking for Colonel Barber?" she asked, tilting her head like Mother Mary.

Speaking for our secret sacred trinity, I stuttered, "Ye-es."

"He's been moved downstairs."

"How do we get there?"

"Follow this aisle to the big white double doors. Make a left and take the elevator to lobby level. He's in 119." She smiled and disappeared down the hall. *All paths to God,* I thought to myself.

The girls and I eyeballed each other, took in three deep breaths, and continued our campaign with a detour to the ground floor. No one said anything to us as we passed through swinging doors and decked down the halls to the right room. When we finally arrived we found the Chaplain's door ajar. Transformed by his past advice we walked through it.

He lay propped up with a pillow beneath his head. His glasses were resting on the tray table beside his bed. It looked like he was sleeping, but I couldn't see his chest rising with every breath he took. His mouth agape was a frightening reminder of my grandfather's last gasp.

With my little girls standing beside me I was transported back in time to my grandfather's dying room.

I saw myself in suffering sorrow, ill-prepared to meet death that night. I wasn't ready to read "Away" or talk with him about any Riley poem of old. I held him and prayed silently, my eyes opened wide inside my mind. Cradled in my arms Grandpa Ted wasn't dead. He looked at me and said, "Everything good is God with an extra 'O' in it."

"*Oh,*" *I said.*

"Oh, my dear, look who's here!" My grandfather's voice became the Chaplain's snapping me back into real time. The Chaplain had opened his eyes and was smiling, glancing all around the room. More than three we were his entire congregation. "How good of you to come."

The girls gathered near his blanketed feet. "We colored cards for you," Mikayla warmed up, defrosting the invisible windows that had trailed in behind.

Her third grade friends had made over thirty special greeting cards detailing their memories of the Chaplain's past visit. The construction paper cards contained messages for a speedy recovery with lots of ice cream. The girls displayed each one for him in art gallery fashion.

He particularly liked the one from Mikayla which pictured a uniformed Chaplain clinging to a big white cross atop a rainbow mountain. "Oh, I like that one. It's me! I'm holding on to the cross. Let's decorate my room here and all like that."

"How's the food here, Chaplain?" I asked him.

"It's not the best mess!"

I gave him an awkward hug over his metal bedrail while the girls reached to squeeze his hands. I set a few of my new business cards next to the TV set on his rolling nightstand. "I took your business card idea to the limit, Chaplain. Here's the *Future-is-now-Me* featured on the front of my card. Listed on the back are the working titles of the book ideas we've talked about."

"How about that," he smiled. "What an interesting idea. See it happen to make it happen. Good for you. Put one up over there on that corkboard. Hang it up high right by that Crayola cross picture."

We fulfilled his request just before the evening nurse found us. She said it was, "Time for the Chaplain's dinner," and we'd, "better be going."

"Onward," I promised him I'd keep researching and writing this book. "I have an appointment tomorrow with your old friends at Park Avenue Christian Church in Montebello. A kind woman there has resurrected two scrapbooks and a church history for me."

"Isn't that something," he said. "I'd like to take a look at that with you. Come back soon."

I glanced at the girls gone ghostly quiet. "We will," I said. Without inciting a riot we slipped out unseen and not forgotten, Chaplain Barber's forever friends, marching ever-onward like little Christian soldiers.

Onward then, ye people, join our happy throng, Blend with ours your voices in the triumph song. Glory, laud and honor unto Christ the King, This through countless ages men and angels sing.

—Final verse, "Onward, Christian Soldiers"
Words: Sabine Baring-Gould, 1865
Music: "St. Gertrude," Arthur S. Sullivan, 1871

X

EYES ON THE CROSS

Rock of Ages, Truth divine, Strong foundation,
ever mine; Safe, secure, I here remain, In the peace
He doth ordain;

— "Rock of Ages" (Words, Anonymous)

ᏬᏒᎪ ᏬᏒᎪ ᏬᏒᎪ ᏬᏒᎪ ᏬᏒᎪ ᏬᏒᎪ ✝ ᎠᏬ ᎠᏬ ᎠᏬ ᎠᏬ ᎠᏬ ᎠᏬ

A prayerful graying lady sat on the water damaged carpet on the floor of the church office. She tenderly sorted used goods and clothing into a system of saggy brown bags lined up in front of her. When the squeaky screen door slammed shut behind my back she looked me over with a kind smile and raised her right arm trembling, slow-motioning me over to see what she had prepared.

Two black scrapbooks bound with satin strings sat still in a plastic-handled paper sack by her side. The books inside weighed heavy like stone tablets. They almost tore through their thin paper holding. As mimely directed, I grabbed hold of the literary load from the bottom. In glad return I nodded *goodbye* to my friendly donor and backed out through the door. I carried the sacred books like bundled twin babies back to my car, cradling them carefully in my arms through the charitable church lot facing Park Avenue.

Over in the park across the street stood Montebello's City War Memorial. The engraved marble-in-cut-stone grandiosed unbeknownst to the handful of hunched teens gathered there to light up, get stoned and strategize leaving their legacies behind on targeted park walls and amphitheatre benches. These were amped, able teens much like the ones I love to teach, to learn from, to inevitably cry over in my changing America where history is written over so everyone has a chance to make change.

My stomach turned in a dark revolution over the growing gap between there and where I walked stretching surreal. Not alone, but a lump sum of one, I slipped, losing momentum in my spiritual vision quest to save precious memories from the Alzheimer's spreading across the land. Off in the delinquent distance faded the memory of Montebello's fallen finest.

Calling on God for backup raised the grace level in me. God granted me clearance with supersonic surges of invisible vigor. *Romans 8:28* stepped up to the plate and ran through all the signs as the generous bag lady lightly lumbered after me. I turned to face the sweet angel in her aging human suit waving a white paper pamphlet in the air. Spelled across the blue sky behind her radiant shine was God's mixed message for me, an airbrushed *SURRENDER JI-NEEL*, in puffy white cloud whisps floating by.

"You might want to look at this," the angel spoke, securing in my bag the brief narrative chronology of the first sixty years of Park Avenue Christian Church. The white flag was a typed ten pages of transcribed materials kept safe over the years by the daughter of a late church historian, collated by the last living church charter member, and synchronized by a random sampling of other Earth angels. It was the handy work of a holy trinity of people who cared. American people. Spiritual prodigies from babies to baptisms, Montebello weddings to missionary send-offs, Tinsel Tea-like charity fundraisers and the Sunday services they made of their quiet lives.

I took a closer look into the eyes of the messenger. Hers were faith healing power windows to the truth that sets us free. In the meeting of our eyes brightened the light of the world reflecting my past. I saw me, a teenage girl gone to the Angels' game. Dad stood by me in the darkened parking lot after the lights went out, steadfast in wait for an autograph from my favorite player.

I saw the all-star, write-in candidate standing in the back of a pickup truck signing every cap and glove and program thrust in his space. On my torn ballot he wrote, *"May God Bless You Always,"* and he scribbled his name and jersey number next to *Romans 8:28,*

And we know that in all things God works for the good of those who love him, who have been called according to His purpose.

Deeper in reflection where I found my spirit restored I wanted God to bless that ballplayer, this luminous angel before me. I wanted God to bless my Dad and my Chaplain's shining soul inside his frailing body. And I asked God, *please,* to bless those misled kids across the street. *Bless the immediate living,* I prayed, *so they may know good is God with an extra 'O' before it is too late.*

I was breathing again, feeling my heart beating inside my chest, speed reading my mind clear. In the blink of an eye I made a tiny telepathic sacred covenant. In this living solemn promise to preserve Park Avenue history I found my fuller faith in keeping all our loved ones safe, alive and forever in written memory.

I heard the angel sing the wisdom of the ages, *Tell it true, red, white and blue.*

"Thank you so much for these collections," I tried to articulate gratitude. "I'll treasure these as my own." Her translucent hand touched mine. Our lifelines intertwined. There was no longer rhyme nor reason to entertain fear of ages or loss of time.

"Take your time," she smiled serene and wished me luck with this writing. If Chaplain Barber walked beside me this day, he'd have said, *"Fine!"* like I surprised myself saying, "May God bless you always." My underdeveloped faith in myself held me spellbound in rediscovery. In finding my own voice I was becoming this writing with wings, a living creation destined to meet the eyes of a nation alive and kicking and screaming under God for which it stands.

When my angel ascended with a piece of my heart I saw in the park across the street the kind of world that would welcome my Chaplain. *What would Jesus do*, next? My *New Testament* beckoned. I searched the sky for the answers and swallowed them whole:

1.   LOVE WRITING WITH ALL YOUR HEART
2.   LOVE YOUR SUBJECT AS YOURSELF

I surrendered to these self-evident truths and drove off into new basic beginnings where Chaplain Barber had set up shop in my soul. I thought to mosey my way toward Rose Hills where I would leave a flower for Grandma Theone, a farewell poem for Grandpa Ted. On this cemetery ridge maybe others would stay for a moment in my time, like Uncle Harry, Grandma's favorite, dressed for an afternoon of P.T. I would tell them about this book, Chaplain Barber's pocket *Bible*, and the lessons I'm learning along this journey. We could have *Old Home Week* in the Garden of Benediction.

Old Home Week denied my Chaplain getting weak. The Chaplain enjoyed *Old Home Week* when he visited Washington D.C. for the President's Inauguration in 2001, the year the odyssey began, the year he shared with me his secrets and precious memories of faith and family, God and war, love and inspirations and visits with friends because he never met a stranger. He told, three times, of the National Presbyterian Church where Dr. L.R. Elson began pastoring after returning from the battlefields of Europe.

Driving through town I reenacted past car-ride conversations with my Chaplain next to me, lessons in postscript. I transcribed the lost tapes in my mind…

JANELLE: Why did you visit the National Presbyterian Church when you were in Washington?

CHAPLAIN: The first officer I ever admired was Chaplain Elson. He was one of the senior Chaplains who later became General Eisenhower's personal Chaplain during the war in Europe. I got to know him quite well. We first met when he came down to my unit, the 11th Horse Cavalry, at the same time his promotion had caught up with him. I was there to pin his Major's leaves on him! He told me, *"Chaplain, we are moving on up!"* He went on up to become one of the most outstanding Chaplains in our history, leading the National Presbyterian Church from 1946 until he retired in 1973 to devote himself to his duties as Chaplain of the United States Senate. He brought Eisenhower to a closer walk with God, baptizing him in the church there in Washington D.C., 1953. He led great leaders, great American families. He led them to lead more meaningful lives of service. What a great man. What a great service, Dr. L.R. Elson. We stayed in touch through the years. Going to that Church that day was like old home week for me.

JANELLE: What about your promotions? Did you *move on up* like Chaplain Elson predicted?

CHAPLAIN: I was promoted to Captain 'long about May or June of 1942, and I remained a Captain all through the war.

JANELLE: Captain Chaplain.

CHAPLAIN: I received citations along the way, a Bronze Star for my service on D-Day. In a military division you have a senior chaplain who is a lieutenant colonel and a deputy chaplain who is a major. The rest are captains and lieutenants below them in rank, and I was the youngest, remember? We never lost our Lt. Colonel or our Major, and thank God for that. I also wanted to stay with the Division, so I remained Captain.

JANELLE: You're a colonel now. How did that happen?

CHAPLAIN: I was promoted to Major after being recalled to service for the Korean War. I was promoted to Lieutenant Colonel after returning from the Korean War. Much later, the U.S. Service Command promoted me to Colonel, which was nice, but to me, rank is not as important as the kind of service you perform. Service matters most. All of us have the power to perform a kind service, a good deed to any child or creation of God. Just think, if every single person went out there and got the job done, what a well- functioning society we would live in.

Spinning since the war on a storefront on Whittier Boulevard was a red, white and blue candy-striped sign spelling out BARBER...

JANELLE: There's Frank's Barber Shop.

CHAPLAIN: That man never charged me a dime for a haircut. He never charged the military. Another man owned the shop and it turned out he was a Baptist preacher too! He always cut my hair for free through the years. Woody was his name.

JANELLE: Chaplain, what would you say to Woody today if he were still inside his shop?

CHAPLAIN: I'd greet him, "Hello there, Friend," and I'd thank him and tell him what a wonderful service he provided in the community. I'd tell him to sit down and write his story too. I'd tell everybody to make an effort to sit down with their friends, people of service in their communities. Write their stories. Preserve the living for history's sake. Tell it true today while the door is still open.

Whenever we merrily rolled along, my Chaplain Barber would sing his fond patriotic soul's sweet song. Led by this presence, power, and peaceful open mind I was enabled to find my way back to his old home to unwind. I slowed for a closer look. There it was painted the same avocado green, secured to the sacred ground on Greenwood where he once reigned supreme. The house was his castle he picked up and hauled to the property purchased with seventeen hundred dollars.

Squinting hard with my spyglass eyes I could barely make out a moving image of my Chaplain, a light being beside his father-in-law working late into the night. And Helen was there with her hands high in the air directing them left and right. I was watching a home movie, black and white.

I remembered our first drive by the house when room edition story ideas inspired inside me. His face lit up like an angel's in a chaplain suit, he was man made young again on Memory Lane working together where God was pleased. Tears streaming down my cheeks churned the sweet buttery emotions of my own fond memories, of avocado green, Grandma and Grandpa and me. I drove faster toward Rose Hills.

Leaning up against the flower shop wall was a wooden wagon wheel which had been there forever weathered and welcoming. I stopped for a rose and paper for the poem. In the back cafe I never knew existed a timeless shopkeeper who made me the world's greatest peanut butter and jelly sandwich on homemade bread like Grandma used to bake. There were secret other ingredients to delight delectable like sliced bananas, plump juicy raisins and sweet golden honey. "Here you go, Honey," said the dark haired woman who made my meal with love something familiar. I liked how her fuscia lipstick lips made, "Honey", my name.

"Honey," the last word my Grandpa Ted said to his beloved before he knew she was gone. I don't think she could have heard him clearly; but I could hear him now, calling out to me in the distant echo of Chaplain Barber's, "Ji-neel!" ringing in my ears.

I followed the voices up the hill, traveling past rows and rows of white crosses and roses. There were dying flowers that knoweth the hours, and Teddy Bear tributes on black marble beauties scoured with names and dates. I carried the remains of my sandwich wrapped inside the red rose arrangement pierced by a pink glittery cross-on-a-stick. The water vase chose to be buried above Grandma below me. I couldn't dig it out so I swept THEONE's name clean with my bare hand on BELOVED, laying to rest her rose and the whirligig cross upon THE ONE AND ONLY. I patted her grave three times.

She gave me the most wonderful hug, *"That's for you,"* she said in the gentle breeze. I saw her, see-through soft, standing by the olive tree. She was pink dress pretty, wearing dainty white gloves waving at me. She blew me a kiss and giggled as Grandpa sat down beside me placing one hand on my shoulder for support. Uncle Harry turned up with a ball and a catcher's mitt, calling me to pitch my hardest to him. His smile was to die for. No wonder he was everybody's favorite.

Long in conversation, prayer and meditation, I became one with God's love for his children and grandchildren growing stronger. With a gentle wave of the hand, Harry wandered again into an unknown land, and Grandma and Grandpa walked hand-in-hand over the hill after him. They left the ball in my court to use in case of emergencies missing them.

I missed them Chaplain Barber style, prideful in my living history. I checked my caller i.d. and found a timed message for me on my cell phone with low battery. I hit 9 to save, 1 to replay. I heard my Chaplain cheerfully say, *"Ji-neel! How are you my dear? Come and see me. You know where I am."* I loved him advancing with technology.

I tumbled down the grassy slope and out of Rose Hills Cemetery, understanding my family wasn't there in the rolling hills where the roses grew. They were right here on the phone, never alone, safe on walks with me. We could meet wherever we chose to be, at any crossroads, or alive and breathing in me.

I knew the Chaplain's Helen really rested somewhere, too, like her *Helen Heaven* and in the many memories of all the lives she touched or knew. I thought of all our spirit allies. One and all experiencing their own soul stories in a place they called their own. A place prepared, by God, for them by them. They could shape it and share it how they wished, like we do here if we want to. In this place they could perform acts of service like they did for me today because I left my door unlocked, wide open. A slice of *Janelle Heaven* because I believe.

Faithfully, I returned my Chaplain's call and set up a friendly visit. We talked about our families and he prophesied to me, "I was talking to the president of Rose Hills Memorial Cemetery the other day and I said to him, '*You know, sir, you are going to be the last man to let me down!*'"

"Funny, that's where I was today, standing next to family in the Garden of Benediction."

"Helen, too! And I'll be there again, next to her one day."

"No, you have to stay."

"Right, okay, I'll stay another day."

"And another. We have so much to do."

"Tell me, how are the girls getting along in their school?"

"Well, I don't know. Little Marlena has had a tough time in first grade. Mikayla seems to be enjoying school, making friends, but they aren't coming home to me the bright cheery children I know." I blanketed.

"Hmm, well, that's not so good," he said.

"I had a strange experience, Chaplain, when my dad and I walked with the girls through their science fair the other night. You know what we saw?"

"What's that?"

"There was a yellow faded, framed proclamation on the multi-purpose room wall with President Ronald Reagan's signature on it. It was the written dedication of the building I was standing in, and right there next to Reagan's fine hand was my father's, the former Mayor."

"How about that! Two of my favorite people left their mark on your children's school!" the Chaplain hoorayed from his bed chambers at the Royal Court.

"I thought it was special too," I concurred, "but what struck me dumbfoundedly is no one else looked where I looked. No one noticed the notice or took to notice. No one cared. And it's such a small town."

"Oh, boy," the Chaplain's voice grew serious.

"Since then," I added, "something has been whirling around me, like winds of change, or a sign." I fished, "What do you think?"

"Ji-neel, a call has been issued to all Baptists, asking them to send their children to private school. That might be something for you to think about."

"But I'm not a Baptist," I reminded him, well aware he was repeating himself.

"But you know God, and everything good that comes from Him."

I thought about that kind reminder. I prayed too, and fast approached Memorial Day 2004, my Chaplain's and my third anniversary. Mikayla and I went to visit our bed-ridden Chaplain in Room 316 to celebrate. We brought him the old Park Avenue package.

"Look-y here! That's me! Oh, that looks like, hey, that might be Helen!" The Chaplain was thrilled.

I pointed out a narrow news clipping, "This article here tells of the flood relief fund you established for the victims up in Northern California at the Weott Christian Church."

"I remember that. Our Sunday School group raised a thousand dollars and we gave it to them in a check. I wore a suit and I delivered it myself. That was a lot of money back then. How about that."

We put the books away and the Chaplain told me about the upcoming D-Day Special Edition of *Time Magazine*. "They interviewed me and I'm going to be in there, you see!" He proudly gleamed pleased to see us, feeling set free to share his good news. "Would you read this here letter for me, dear?" he handed me a Xeroxed copy of a letter from Congressman Ed Royce who was up for re-election this year.

"I'd be glad to, Chaplain. It says,

Dear Mr. Barber,

As Memorial Day approaches, we are reminded of the brave men and women who served our country courageously in World War II.

For years, WWII Veterans and their families have never had a Memorial to honor their service and their sacrifices. The World War II Memorial has finally been established for this purpose and will be dedicated on May 29th, 2004.

I regret that you are unable to attend the dedication event. However, I would like to take this opportunity to commend you for your dedication and service to our country. I am honored to know that men like you have defended and protected our country.

Again, thank you for your patriotic service. If I can ever be of assistance to you, please feel free to contact my district office.

Sincerely,
Edward R. Royce
Fortieth District-California."

"How about that," the Chaplain sighed a happy smile and asked me to pin the letter on his wall next to the picture of his granddaughter's new baby.

"Mom?" Mikayla mumbled from her crouching tiger position. She pinned herself down against the wall fleeing the groping hand of a demented old woman who had wheeled herself into to the hall of the Chaplain's quarters.

"Whoa, wait a minute here!" I raised my voice to the hellcat the Chaplain could not see.

"What's going on?" He tried to help.

The wild woman frighteningly widened her fixed gaze upon my daughter and cackled, "I know who you are! I'm going to fix you up right!"

Just then a scrubbed orderly grabbed hold of the handles on the hell-bent woman's wheelchair and whisked her away while she cursed and clenched her fists.

"I'm so sorry," he said in corn-sweetened Spanish. "She does this all the time." He looked down at Mikayla who bore the look of horror on her little creampuff face. He asked, "Are you okay? Did she touch you?"

"I'm fine," Mikayla said staring straight into my eyes a message of, "God," and she burst out laughing into tears.

"Laughter is the best medicine!" the Chaplain remedied within earshot.

"I think we'd better go. It's getting late," I suggested.

"It's never too late," Chaplain Barber reminded. "You keep writing and bringing me the good news. I'll be here. Take these chocolates too. I can't eat 'em." He handed me gold paper-wrapped chocolate truffles. "And this book, take this too." It was Louis Zamperini's autobiography, a gripping true story of a POW's spiritual transformation from tortured captive to born again Christian. "You ought to read it," he said.

I promised I would in a kiss on his head and another on his unshaven cheek. His hair wasn't cropped clean and neat as it used to be. I thought, *If only Woody the barber were here.* Maybe he was. Perhaps he arrived just in time for Old Home Week.

When we *talked and talked and talked* again it seemed like a dream of the future past, face-to-face.

CHAPLAIN: Ji-neel, you know what today is?

JANELLE: It's D-Day.

CHAPLAIN: June the Sixth, sixty years ago today, I landed on Omaha Beach. Fifteen hundred and thirty-one of my men died there on the beach that day. And now President Reagan, one of the greatest of my generation, has gone on to join them. The golden gates of Heaven have opened up to his sunset and he is riding through.

JANELLE: Who do you think you'll meet when you get to Heaven?

CHAPLAIN: Helen. And Jesus. I think we get to meet those we love.

JANELLE: What about all your men and all those you served?

CHAPLAIN: It's going to be quite a reunion up there! Like *Old Home Week.*

JANELLE: Do you think we will recognize our loved ones?

CHAPLAIN: Oh, sure we will. We call our loved ones "loved ones" because love is what we know best about them. More than what people look like physically, we feel what we feel towards them. When you love someone and someone loves you, you feel love reciprocating and that's unique for every relationship. Each of our loved ones gives us a different special feeling. I believe we will recognize that feeling first. That's how we will find each other.

JANELLE: What do you say to the common idea that we all get young again and beautiful and radiant, looking our best or our happiest in Heaven?

CHAPLAIN: That's what love does. I think more than being young again and good looking, we will become our love. That is what makes us so special here too, you see.

JANELLE: Our love? But God is love.

CHAPLAIN: He created us in His image.

JANELLE: We are like God?

CHAPLAIN: We must strive to be like God, always and in all ways. We do this by giving love, by being loving. Love comes back, you know.

JANELLE: How do we know we will go to Heaven?

CHAPLAIN: Everybody who loves God and understands

that God loves everybody will go to Heaven.

JANELLE: I sometimes ask myself, *Are you ready? Are you happy now? Are you satisfied with how you've lived your life?* What would you say to these?

CHAPLAIN: I think I'm satisfied. I like to think I have given love all my life in all the things I've done. I know I've tried. And I love everybody. I like some people more than others. Just like I love the Presidents. I have served God under the leadership of eleven different Presidents. I loved them all and prayed for them all, but I liked some better than others.

JANELLE: Who was your favorite?

CHAPLAIN: I love the one we've got now. I've also got a special place in my heart for President Eisenhower. So many aspects of my life connect to these two. But I prayed for each and every one. We must pray for those who lead us and those who serve.

JANELLE: There's no harm in that.

CHAPLAIN: Prayer has never hurt anyone. I wish more people would accept that.

JANELLE: If you had just one wish for the world, what would that be?

Before he answered I drifted away to the day we were on our way to March Air Force Base, the site of his Vietnam War service with the 452nd. Any coincidence it is the same Air Reserve Wing of my father? The retired officers' meeting we missed, but I got to watch the Chaplain in his prideful prime talking with pilots and lingering party guests, "On the Sunday before D-Day I preached on eleven different ships in Weymouth Harbor..."

He signed pocket *Bibles* for his newest congregation of reserve officers, mechanics and mess hall masons. Later that long ago evening we enjoyed, "Fine!" base dining at Hap Arnold's Restaurant, the last supper we shared before the Chaplain's hospitalization.

He ordered steaks for us. When our waitress walked by with a condiment tray for the table across from us, the Chaplain whispered to me, "I never doctor a good steak. There are worms in the mix, and sugar. Ketchup is a candy-coated food addiction."

"Some say we are what we eat," I said.

"So I keep it simple with no sauce."

That night over plain juicy steak and mashed potatoes, buttered bread and wine, I asked him,

"If you had one wish for the world what would it be?"

In his hospital bed he answered with sheer possibility in his eyes, "I wish the whole world would come together in peace and harmony and service to one another."

"Do you think there is any way that could happen?" I doubted.

"I truly believe there will always be hope in this world if we do our job right. If we care for one another by ministering, preaching the gospel of Christ, by living a life of service like God would want us to live. If people have a chance to hear the truth, they will know God and understand how simple it can be to love and be loved. "After I ended the war with Patton down in

Czechoslovakia, I met up with a couple of Polish officers. They said to me, 'Chaplain, come with us for little R & R. We want to take you to a place we think you will like.'

"They invited me to join them in a climb up the tallest peak in Germany, in the Zuspitch Mountains. There were cables already there so we used them to pull ourselves up, hand over hand, to the top of the mountain. The weather was a little frightening, windy and stormy. I was not feeling secure on my feet, but when we reached the top, guess what we found up there? A great big white cross. The cross of Jesus. It was one of the holiest moments of my life.

"When the wind picked up it threw me off balance, and I was way up there. I quickly grabbed 'hold of that cross. All of us did, for dear life. I hung on and I prayed and in that moment I realized this was the message I would carry all the days of my life.

"Several things ran through my mind as I clung to the cross. One was, *In the storms of life, what better thing to hold onto than the cross of Jesus?* And we had seen some pretty rough storms on Omaha Beach. The second thought was, *What better place for the people of the world than to meet under the feet of Jesus right here at the cross?*

"I thought of all the stories of love and help and service to others that Christ shared with us. The cross is the symbol of God's love for us. The love of God is the only thing, really, that will bind the people of the world.

"Think about it, if you love your neighbor, you're not going to steal from him or loot his business or hate him. You're going to do good, you see. So you will always be able to find me clinging on to that cross of Jesus there on the top of the mountain."

The Chaplain saw my tears and handed me a tissue from

the folded pile on his bed stand. I fanned my flushed cheeks and declared, "Your story of the cross is a monument to all Chaplains, to all of us, all one, the perfect symbol to carry the true message and meaning of being a soldier of God."

Hanging in there on the Fourth of July the Chaplain called to say, "Hi, this is your Chaplain speaking. Happy Independence Day. Today is a special day. Good is everywhere and good things are going to happen. Come see me. You know where I am."

At the Fourth of July family block party in my old neighborhood, the Chaplain's message rang true. An angel on crutches named Verna, whose name means *Truth*, brought both the girls a yellow invitation to attend Vacation Bible School at her Holy Cross Church. At one tenth the price of horse camp, I rejoiced in the savings, and the girls spent a summer's week learning Bible verses, *"Halleluiah,"* songs and Jesus stories. They made new friends and came home happy humming hymns.

"Marlena! Mikayla!" I chanted to my girls, "You're on a mission from God!" They tickled me silly with thanks for a week I never would have thought to plan for them on my own.

After they started school in the Fall I called the Chaplain on his new cell phone, a 90th birthday present from his adoring son. He answered on the first ring. I told my Chaplain that God was back in the classroom for my children's sake. "How about that!" he shouted with glee. "Halleluiah! The truth has set you free!"

"It's not free, Chaplain. It's private school and there is a fee."

"Don't worry about how much it costs. You are in the right place and God knows it. He will take care of you. Have faith in that," he promised. "How do the girls like it?"

I hadn't thought past my own selfish needs until he asked me that question. "They are smiling wide and bright," I confirmed.

"Mikayla's on the basketball team. On her jersey is a holy cross with a silver lining."

"Nice," noticed the Chaplain.

"And Marlena has already memorized her part in the chapel play."

"Fan-tastic!"

"Guess what happened on the day I attended the first parent-teacher conference?"

"Tell me."

"Chaplain, my children's teachers prayed for them. The first thing they did to start our meeting was pray for my children."

"Right, good and fine! Now what about you? Have you met anybody yet?"

This question quivering in my ears, the retelling of an earlier prediction, made me mutter, "Funny you should ask that today."

"Oh?"

"Oh, yes," I openly admitted there was a new man in my life.

"How'd you meet him?"

"When in the midst of quick-stop shopping for shelving, dinner, and a storage shed, the girls and I met this nice man at Home Depot."

"A carpenter's dream!" the Chaplain cheered. "Tell me about him."

"He wore King George's red cross printed bold across his shirt chest. On his arm was the image of the Royal Marine commando. Bravo-Two-Zero, British war hero, a member of the allied forces!"

"The girls were with you? What did they think?"

"They begged me to stay and talk with him so they could hear his funny accent. I watched them watch his breathing cross, and I handed him my Chaplain-inspired business card."

"Good for you. Has he called?"

"We've already met for coffee," I confessed.

"Well, I'd like to meet him. Bring him to me. Let me check him out. I like the English. You know I was in England when Winston Churchill was voted out of office. Can you believe it? Winston Churchill was voted out of office! Not enough people paid attention and just like that, the best leader they ever had was out of power. I talked to some folks there who were just devastated. We can't let that happen here. Are you registered to vote?"

"Of course! I'm a woman. No woman should ever shirk her responsibility to exercise her hard fought right to vote."

"Amen to that!"

"Amen, my Chaplain."

"Well, I love you, Dear."

"I love you, too."

Two books I bought from the children's two-for-one book fair lay at my feet on the floor. On top was *Walt Whitman: Words for America*, a gorgeous tribute to America's poet by Barbara Kerley with illustrations by Brian Selznick. It was juvenile literature for everyone, a must read that led me to explore so much more. In reading Walt Whitman I saw all along, Chaplain Barber's long life of service to soldiers by his side. Both these men of service loved their President, personally, strong.

From the bulletin board altar above my desk the Chaplain's eyes sparkled approvingly at me. As I keyed each letter into my machine, *O' Chaplain! My Chaplain! Man of Service* rose consciously to life.

I invited Walt Whitman into the room, great ghost and writer friend. He guided me along with God's blessings in bold, keeping watch while I wondered. I digressed, trying to guess if reincarnation were ever part of God's subplotting bests.

Chaplain Barber, soldier of God, began speaking to me from the podium on my homespun shrine. The words challenged me much like his work gripping audiences at other gatherings, making His word last. He said,

"With the birth of a little baby boy this morning in Beslan, there are over six billion mouths to feed in the world today. You can live nearly forty days without food, but you can only live seven days without water. Today we need to make sure there is clean water all over the world. Shelter. Clothing. Schools.

"We are challenging all those who have money and all those who have power and all the churches and good organizations to come together to help make this world a safe place to live. A place for freedom. A Heaven on Earth. May it be a place beloved by all as it is beloved by Christ the King."

Walt Whitman wrote, *"The chief reason for the being of the United States of America is to bring about the common good will of all mankind, the solidarity of the world."* To me he said, *"I place my hand upon you,"* and into the night and straight on 'til morning, I became his poem.

On this poem night, my students playfully candied my house with sweets and treats and balloons on strings, I volunteered my classic car for the Veterans' Day Parade, and I reached the end of tapes...

JANELLE: Chaplain, I've got a few more questions.

CHAPLAIN: Shoot.

JANELLE: If we get to our Heaven, and we meet our loved ones again, and we are brought before God. What will happen next?

CHAPLAIN: When we face the King of Kings in the end of days, He's not going to ask any theological questions, and aren't you glad about that? But you'll be there on the right and here's what He is going to say, He's going to say, *"For I was hungry and you gave me something to eat, I was thirsty and you gave me something to drink, I was a stranger and you took me in,"* He's going to remind us of all the good works we did without even thinking we were doing good. Like my teacher with her sweater. And your teacher with his *Carl's Jr* lunch. You with the children you serve. You will get to have your Heaven too. I'd like to know about your idea of Heaven, Ji-neel.

JANELLE: Something tells me I'm going to meet the smoking woman from La Palma!

CHAPLAIN: That's good. Take her by the hand. What else?

JANELLE: I'd like to wander with Walt Whitman, my poetic Santa Claus.

CHAPLAIN: O good! Go on...

JANELLE: I'd like to play catch with Uncle Harry and go fishing on the Lewis River without a license. I'd like to sit at the feet of Grandpa Ted as he smokes his pipe and blows smoke rings between readings of his favorite stories to his children and grandchildren. *Janelle Heaven* will have poetry and good books and children playing, children laughing. I will walk with my Collies and Great Uncle Irv through the woods along Cole Witter Road. My mother and I won't cry anymore over Grandma Theone because she won't be gone, she'll be there, giggling and singing silly songs, my hands on her hands across piano keys. No business will be left unfinished, or if it is, it won't matter anymore.

CHAPLAIN: Why don't you read and write, drum and play, and walk each way with this kind of emotion right now? Enjoy life. God wants you to be happy right now. He's glad to be alive in you. It's important you get to go to Heaven, but have a little slice of it wherever you go today. Live! And while you're at it, love! Listen. Learn. Believe.

JANELLE: I have an old bookstore friend I like to visit on the Seal Beach pier. We sit and talk on his memorial bench with those same words written in dedication.

CHAPLAIN: And how did I know that?

JANELLE: Because you are my Chaplain.

CHAPLAIN: Ji-neel, this has been such a great adventure, such a good walk. To you and all who read this I hope and pray that my life and experiences grip your heart and soul so that you will love God and Christ and give your life in love and service to others.

JANELLE: You have taught me so much.

CHAPLAIN: First thought, best thought, what is the one thing you have learned that you will carry with you all the days of your life?

JANELLE: I will no longer mourn in death, but celebrate life, including the one I'm in.

CHAPLAIN: And those you meet will know who you are, child of God.

JANELLE: Changed in you. I am your good act of service.

CHAPLAIN: Ji-neel, you have served me well in kind.

JANELLE: And if you leave me behind I will find you on the mountain top, holding on to the cross. I'll keep my eyes always meeting yours there.

CHAPLAIN: *Surely goodness and love will follow you all the days of your life and you will dwell in the house of the Lord forever.*

TITHES AND OFFERINGS

"It is by grace you have been saved,
Through faith—and this not from yourselves,
it is the gift of God."

—Ephesians 2:8

ᚢᚱᚢᚱᚢᚱᚢᚱᚢᚱᚢᚱ ✝ ᚫᚢᚫᚢᚫᚢᚫᚢᚫᚢᚫᚢ

God gives gifts in many different packages. For example, things that happen to us are in most cases happening for us, thanks to God. This simple concept when applied teaches me the reason I "just happened" to be there the night my grandfather passed away. God chose me. I met Chaplain Barber on Memorial Day the same way. Life was happening to me, for me.

God never asked me for recognition on either occasion. He only continued to make subtle suggestions, recommendations on where to go next. He sent me my guides to give me hot tips in my dreams. I believe He sent me hints and clues in many forms, hoping I'd find my true path. There were accidents and illnesses, emotional rollercoaster rides, event after event to create waves of change. I rode the current and finally got current, following the energy flow without judgment to wind up here having my life.

For over three years this book has been one of the most important love relationships of my life. Now it is my eternal give away, in service to Chaplain Barber, for the young men he served on D-Day, in memory of all who served, for you, for me, for God. It is a spiritually bilingual thank you letter, begun in *Sorrowful Soul* transformed into *Joyful Heart*. Both are love languages that have served me well. Perhaps we should all consider giving of ourselves, paying our tithes and offering up our unique specialties in service to others.

Acts of kindness are acts of recovery. We must not engage with outcomes in mind, looking to get something back. Somewhere in human training there developed an idea that giving would be good because we could write it off, save on taxes, get our name on a tile or emblazoned on a plaque. That's all fine and dandy, but more important is the nature of giving.

Giving is a divine rite of passage. I say, "rite it off" as the right thing to do, no matter what you give or what you can do, as long as it serves humanity, with humility, like the good Chaplain's good news.

Along the course of this study, I participated in many events that involved giving. I noticed some people giving in pain. These were often the ones with more power to give, intimidating those with a different gift. This created more pain and gave giving a bad name. A negative charge. This can give cause to chase people away from giving altogether.

Looking at service altruistically is the key. Giving should not be painful or intimidating or manipulative. It should be joyful, kind, feel-good and fun. Generosity, like God, can come in many mysterious ways. Giving, like God, can be interpreted in many different languages at many different levels. A gift does not have to compare with anyone or anything else, so make it your own. Make it unique. In this vein, your gift may inspire more giving.

There are many ways to serve that don't have to include money, but if you have it, give a dollar. Give whatever you can afford in service to someone. If you choose to give money, give wisely. Some say ten percent is the right ratio. What matters most is the feeling or the energy that comes with it.

Ten cents to someone who only has a dollar is a large chunk of change. Appreciate that change. Without change there can be no growth. Every little bit counts.

From my *experience* I've found as long as the gift comes with love, without pain or worry, it is good to give it. Like the more love you give, the more love you feel. Love attracts love. A wise man once said to me, "As you think, so shall you attract." I imagine if you think positive thoughts, positive things will follow. Be open to that possibility. There is power in possibility, and positive thinking helps.

If money is what you have to give, Chaplain Barber has hundreds of connections with worthy organizations all over the world who would do good work with your donation. Make contact. Seek them out. Read about them. Listen. Love. Learn. (*Reference Study Guide*)

Colin Powell's *America's Promise* always promises to deliver. *Assist Ministries* does wonderful work. They are also connected with *Russian Ministries* who can really use your help right now. *Angeles Crest Christian Camp* could always use a helping hand. Keep campers camping and join the fun. Invest in the future of future gift-givers.

I would love to list all of the Chaplain's chosen contacts, but there are more pages in Chaplain Barber's little black book than there are in this work in publication. By checking back with the website, *www.livingdday.com* from time to time you will find Chaplain Barber's bright ideas and suggestions for making donations, volunteering, giving of yourself in service. We will be eternally mixing the ingredients for his recipe of service.

For now, here are a few more thoughts to ponder: "Money, money, money," says the Chaplain, "you can't take it with you, but you can't go anywhere in this world without it." Money talks with the Chaplain taught me these three things,

1.   Manage money wisely so gift–giving won't break my bank.

2.   Use common sense.

3.   Help where help is needed.

A multi-tasking single mom understands that money is tight most of the time. Giving money might not always be the way to serve. Instead, give some time. My girls and I tried *Christmas Boxes* with *Samaritan's Purse*. This is a fun, organized, worthy cause.

If time is of the essence, give a little of yourself. Everyone has a talent. Teach it. Everyone has a gift. Give it. These are simple ways to serve others in a world that really needs help. Just yesterday my neighbor lent me his jumper cables and helped me get my old car started. Be a good neighbor, simple, effective kindness.

My relationship with the Chaplain often sent me reeling over the way our nation's veterans have been left to fend for themselves. It's been getting better over the years, but it's still not where it needs to be. Go visit a veterans home or hospital. Take a veteran to lunch or to see a memorial. The Seal Beach Pier features one of the most memorable of memorial markers. Go see it. "Take a walk. Have a talk," says the Chaplain.

Get involved with Operation Homefront. "Sometimes," he continues, "if we look no further than our own backyards, our families, neighbors, friends, we'll find people who served, who wore the uniform for this country, the women who went into the factory, those who toed the line. Kindly thank them for the contribution they made. Help those serving today."

The night I was ordained I met Ralph Ramirez who leads the California Military History Museum's *Oral History Project*. This is a fantastic educational program using stories told by the service men and women who made history happen. This, and other work like it, serves to preserve the memories of our loved ones so they may live forever like we've always wished for. Contact Ralph or seek for yourself a story that moves you. Record someone's story. What if you were there? Record your own life story like Bob Searl has done online. Serving yourself could be serving generations to come. Ponder if you will, then contact the National D-Day Memorial Foundation with your donation. Give story, give time, give energy, give love, give to educate the future caring adults of America. Honor the past, savor today, light the way for a better tomorrow.

After you study Chaplain Barber's business card and the New Testament he may have given you, he recommends you read a book called *Volunteering: 101 Ways You Can Improve the World and Your Life* by Douglas M. Lawson. This book can help you find a way to serve that makes sense to you, something that is comfortable and fits your lifestyle. If you can't buy the book, check it out at the library or go online. There are so many ways to be of service and it doesn't have to cost money.

If you love animals, visit an animal shelter. If you are a breed-specific dog or cat lover, most breeds have rescue organizations ready and waiting for volunteers. I have two collies saved by

Southland Collie Rescue who are simply the most wonderful creatures known to woman. They ooze love, and you can too when you volunteer.

After my first Christmas with the Chaplain, I started receiving a multitude of magazines and periodicals in my mail. I couldn't remember subscribing to anything or putting my name on any lists, but I didn't toss them aside. Remaining open to possibility and reserving judgment, I tried reading them for myself. Coincidentally, they were the same materials the Chaplain subscribes to: *Christianity Today, Decision, Imprimus, Focus on the Family, The Washington Times* and *Guideposts*. The Chaplain waited several issues before asking me, "How are you getting along with your reading?" The selfless giver in him touched my heart. I read on smiling gratefully.

Combined with *The Daily Word* and Mikayla's *Horses*, gifts in previous years from other kind people, I found these materials to be of good service. In the least, they didn't hurt. Moreover, I found they provide spiritual food for the hungry reader, and thought-provoking questions for the non-believer. (Horses, by the way, are the most spiritual of all God's land animals, then come dogs, then come the cats.)

In my travels with Chaplain Barber I was often awed by the humanity in the rooms we visited. One room was filled with doctors and business leaders, spiritual teachers, givers of time, money, talent and research for *AIDS Project Liberia*, an altruistic organization serving a continent in crisis.

These people, and people like them, are rarely seen in the news because they give quietly, concentrating their time and energy on getting their work done. Public accolade could take away from their work. Because they are selfless in their cause and devoted to taking grueling and busying action, there is no time to toot a horn or host a dinner.

Another friend of Chaplain Barber's, Frank Kaleb Jansen, created a simple way to re-educate the people of war-torn nations like Afghanistan and Iraq. He put it all in a box. Nice packaging. Easy opening. Oddly, no one has taken the time or energy to back this man's genius plan at the time of this printing. Maybe YOU will help promote Jansen's education-in-a-box idea and see it through to fruition. Send your idea to Chaplain Barber via www.livingdday.com. He will try to put you in touch with the right "mover" or "shaker" depending on the genre.

Don't be afraid to bring your own good ideas to the table. Anything that is good comes from God. That includes God in you, working through you. Service is performance art, creation. Silver lining shines when your work comes from a selfless heart of divine goodness. Hearts young and old have a vein of gold. This is the brilliant path that leads to a life of service. Here, love happens.

Says the Chaplain, "For more ways to serve others," *or maybe it was FOUR more ways...*

1. Communicate Christ's love to everyone.
2. Live by Christ's example.
3. Love God with all your heart.
4. Love your neighbor as yourself.

Some may ask, *"How do I love my neighbor when my neighbor does not love?"* or *"How do I love my neighbor when my neighbor hurts me intentionally?"*

Understand that God does not hurt intentionally or perpetuate anything unloving. Humans carry that capacity just as we carry the capacity to love. You can still like who you want when you love everybody.

We are all suffering from the pains of our past. Some suffer an imbalance by becoming their pain, which can cause pain in others. This does not have to become any of us. If heavy burden begins to shift or weigh you down, let go and let God in you. Honor the God in your heart by learning to forgive. This is what good people need to do. General Bradley did this. We may have won the war and changed the world because of it.

For a deeper understanding of forgiveness, the Chaplain recommends you help yourself to reading Devil at my Heels by Louis Zamperini with David Rensin. This book serves up a heaping, overwhelming helping of human triumph through God's love and power over evil. It details the life of a man who endured torturous human cruelty, worse-than-fatal wartime danger, and offers an unforgettable ray of hopeful-heart conquest in the form of forgiveness, the non-fiction metaphor for a happy ending. Read it and weep until you find God's love in you.

Trace the clues in your own life to find your true path. In the quest for truth and justice regarding my grandmother's unsolved murder I found Jannel Rap. Synchronicity! Another "Ji-neel!" This Jannel is a native Nebraskan. She is a talented folk singer/songwriter whose sister, Gina Bos, disappeared nearly four years ago, leaving small children without a mom. Jannel's perseverance, her torch leading the search for her sister, moved her to create G.I.N.A., *Greater Information Now Available*. Likewise, she sponsors and promotes the television program *Missing in America*, a reach out to cable viewers who may help.

Jannel donates her time, talent and energy through music, in a valiant effort to find answers to the mysterious questions that riddle law enforcement and survivors of the lost. Look her up. Go see her play. Buy her very affordable cds. Imagine. While enjoying yourself with good music you could help generate awareness which could lead to locating a missing person.

"There is so much to do," the Chaplain concludes. If you are having trouble deciding what to do, ask God to guide you. Chaplain Barber and I agree you will find yourself where you need to be. While you search for what works for you, whatever you may choose to do, ever-well-wishes. May you walk in the beauty of a silver lining as you kindly serve. And you never know, if you attend the meeting of the eyes with the next person you serve, there may be many happy returns.

BENEDICTION

*O Lord my God, When I in awesome wonder
Consider all The works Thy Hand hath made,
I see the stars, I hear the mighty thunder,
Thy pow'r Throughout The universe displayed;
Then sings my soul, My Saviour God, to Thee,
How great Thou art! How great Thou art!*

—Carl G. Boberg, 1885
English tr. Stuart K. Hine

ᏌᎳᏌᎳᏌᎳᏌᎳᏌᎳᏌᎳ ✝ ᎠᏧᎠᏧᎠᏧᎠᏧᎠᏧᎠᏧ

Dear God,

How great Thou art. I thank You that I have been privileged to serve You as a chaplain in five wars, touching the lives of hundreds of thousands of military personnel around the world. I thank You for allowing me to preach the gospel of love in Your Church for over 70 years. I thank You for my family and friends.

You have guided me to help people in a humanitarian field working with more than a hundred organizations and to have a part in the rescue of orphaned children. It has been my privilege to have been a consultant in the fields of energy, education, finance, communication, business, health, food and clean water in working with spiritual leaders all over the world.

I thank You for these blessings. I thank You now and forever more. *Amen and amen.*

Colonel Chaplain George Russell Barber

LET US PRAY

Of all my meetings, event-attendings and interviews with Chaplain Barber, the most meaningful moments were the prayers. Always simple. Always true. No matter where we had gathered ourselves together we could be found praying. We prayed in my car in the parking lot of *Jack's*, sometimes daring to disciple while driving to an event.

Whenever I called on the Chaplain, he immediately called on the Lord. We prayed before each recording, during and after too. We prayed over meals. We prayed over the phone, Chaplain Barber's spirit in spoken word while I listened with all my heart at home. The spontaneous break-into-prayers, at first I found so funny. They moved right in next to God becoming permanent residents in the bottom of my heart.

For these reasons alone I declare we need a middle-man in our lives once in a while, someone to guide us on our walk in life. By shedding my past as he told his story, I have surely grown. In prayerful moments over the phone, in our corner booth, or at red lights changing green, my spirit has soared. It is dim no more. Because of this I am a better me. The *Me* I am supposed to be.

With this book *experience*, which has prepared me for the next, I learned that goodness comes from God with an extra

'O' that never rests. I hope my children and their children will understand this test. With every ounce of pain can come power. From out our sorrow can spring our best.

Chaplain Barber was never bothered when no babysitter was secured to care for my girls. Instead, he silently suggested it was something God did to me, for me, for him and them as well.

In together days we shaped our history in simple ways. In meditative afterglow I found new interpretations to the answers I held all along: I love God with all my heart. I love my neighbor as myself, especially Chaplain Barber. This meditation melded a good gift with its Giver, a one-of-a-kind pleasure prayer I will cherish forever:

> *The Lord is my Shepherd, I shall close my eyes to see my girls sitting next to me wearing Jesus shoes. Their sweet sandaled feet stick-slide across orange vinyl. They settle down to color kid menus in the corner booth at Jack's. The sun is setting over their shoulders as they nibble on cracker snacks.*

> *Chaplain Barber, suited for service in his modern Air Force uniform, offers one gentle hand to each of them. I nudge Marlena and give a nod to her sister. It's time to take hold of him now.*

> *They bow their heads and eye each other reverently wiggling. Mikayla closes her eyes. Marlena sighs. Both hush to hear our Chaplain give loving thanks for, "…this meal and this blessed time together in Jesus' name. Amen."*

> *My soul shifts gears to rejoice through tears how*

blessed we are to be here. My still small voice
says soft and slow, "Chaplain Barber is the
most spiritually decorated man I know." While
his memories thrive and he strives to tell us, he
decorates our lives eternally blessed.

In this knowing comes to mind my Grandpa's favorite poems, memories free-flowing. My heartlight shines ever-glowing when I hear his spirit read to me. I hope and pray that before the end of days I will get to say all that needs to be. We have so much to do, my Chaplain. Please don't ever leave.

I don't want to read that Riley poem of old, but when it's time I'll try it just for you. There will be no pressure. I'll pause and gesture like Grandpa Ted used to do. It will all be okay. Somehow, some way, with you in my sight forever, I'll make it turn out right. On that night or during that day, I will wish you stood beside me. I'll feel you there and what I share might sound something like this,

"AWAY"

I can not say and I will not say
That he is dead.-He is just away!

With a cheerful smile, and a wave of
          the hand,
He has wandered into an unknown land,

And left us dreaming how very fair

It needs must be, since he lingers
          there.

And you-O you, who the wildest
        yearn
For the old-time step and the glad return,-
Think of him faring on, as dear
In the love of There as the love of
        Here;

And loyal still, as he gave the blows
Of his warrior-strength to his country's foes.-
Mild and gentle, as he was brave,-
When the sweetest love of his life he
        gave
To simple things:-Where the violets
        grew
Blue as the eyes they were likened to,

The touches of his hands have strayed
As reverently as his lips have prayed:
When the little brown thrush that
        harshly chirred
Was dear to him as the mocking-bird;
And he pitied as much as a man in
        pain
A writhing honey-bee wet with rain.-
Think of him still as the same, I say:
He is not dead- he is just away!

—James Whitcomb Riley

October is *Clergy Appreciation Month* every year. Chaplain Barber is my pastor. The work my pastor has put into God's plan for his long life has often gone unseen or unrecognized even by those of us who know him well. Every October, every year, every day and evermore, I plan to celebrate my pastor. With this manuscript I say, "Thank you," for the many ways my pastor serves me, my little girls, my community, America's Veterans, our world. I pray today that with this work he will know how much he is cherished and treasured.

There is a message for me in the simple math of this work of service. After adding up all the time we have spent together -lessons I've learned walking with him, meals I've enjoyed sitting by his side, the many prayers we've prayed, all the times I beat myself up, the buckets of tears I've filled, miles I've driven, dreams I've had, pens I've lost, paper wads I've shot into the recycle bin, and the many times I carried and searched through that overflowing, grey tattered briefcase for stuff, for him, for Him- I come out a billionaire, brimming with love's spinning.

I'm so heaped in countless blessings I'm heavy in heart and bursting to go gift-giving. Love, love, love! Love for everyone. Love especially for God's special guest speaker, Colonel Chaplain George Russell Barber, the last living D-Day chaplain from the landing at Omaha Beach. I am recovered in him. Him. I could sing a hymn. Acts of kindness breed speedy recovery.

Pass it on.

Amen.

MEMORIAL DAY

Happy Birthday to You!
Happy Birthday to You!
Happy Birthday, Dear Ji-nee-eel!
Happy Birthday to You!

-Chaplain Barber
March 11th, 2005

It was March 11th, the annual date to commemorate my arrival on this living planet. The year was 2005, a time for healing. A ritual free-will walk in renewal. My special day would begin with resistance, me being the Me I was meant to be. I was fallen on my knees grieving on a grassy slope overlooking Hillside Chapel where Chaplain Barber's life had been celebrated just a few months before.

On this my 38th birthday, I selfishly longed for my genteel Georgia gentleman to sing to me the Ji-neel Birthday Jingle over the phone. But it didn't happen. My Chaplain had already gone home. To Helen. And Jesus. To *Chaplain Heaven* where his work would never be done.

Locked inside my miserable painbody I recollected quiet visits when he lay dying and I defended against crying, and he held this manuscript in his trembling hands. Minus this chapter, he read it through several times and shared his approval with me. In our final moments together he squeezed my hand and said,

"You've done well." He pulled me closer and carefully instructed, "Now spread the word, to hundreds, thousands of 'em."

I kissed his dry lips and made that promise. "I will see you again soon," I said, the night before he died.

I felt like I had lied in the lagging months after his passing. These became my mourning pages where writing and sobbing became twin souls. Like the book had become him I held onto it more tightly and covetously. It was mine to have and to hold, to never grow old, to crumple and tear, paper shoulders to cry all over and swear. I wasn't serving them well.

Not until this birthday of rebuilding, the day I would dare to raise new death and resurrection questions, would I learn to set *My Chaplain* free. In letting him go I would find him again, standing right beside me, back to tell me more.

At Rose Hills where I took refuge in my lonely birthday distance I watched other mourners slowly milling about Hillside Chapel. Softly through the trees there came a gentle breeze blowing memories into my needy ears. I could almost hear us talking. Musical voices, like delicate hands-over-hands across piano keys, were Chaplain Barber's loved ones celebrating his life of ninety years that touched us all so deeply.

Memorial day moments slide-showed across my mind's eye movie screen. Risen to the podium was Larry Keene sharing Psalm 23, and his wife, Virginia, singing favorite church hymns in joyful reverie. There were stories of George Russell Barber signing pocket Bibles as if he alone had authored them! Many laughed at the father and grandfather who proudly inserted his business card into every family holiday greeting. Holy rolling stories about this man of service we remembered fondly forever, like the Bible on the beach.

Barely breathing I could not read "Away" that Riley poem of

old. Instead, I chose memories of my proud friend of Biblical proportions who knew all along we were on a mission from God. I confessed I missed him more than blessings untold. And like a knock on the door, this reflection show sharply stopped. My body lunged forward. In a dizzying way, on my knees I prayed aloud to God and the man who wasn't there, "Where do I go from here?"

Facing my fear, "O Chaplain! My Chaplain!" I cried. "Please believe me, I've tried."

Fallen by his graveside, I bowed my head low and heavy, giving to God the pieces of my broken heart meant soul-ly for mending. I prayed like everything was up to Him to heal me, and I spoke to the last living D-Day Chaplain of Omaha Beach like he was listening.

"Chaplain Barber?" I pleaded, "Are you there?"

My heart suddenly beat fast-forward in a fight against the rhythm of the Earth. Pounding feet were sounding off, loud and clear in my right ear, all that they were worth. With my eyes forced firmly closed, I formed a moving image of the Chaplain in my mind. In this magical march to where he lay sleeping and I was blessed to go on living, I heard him sing to me...

CHAPLAIN: Happy birthday to you! Happy birthday to you! Happy birthday, dear Ji-nee-eel, happy birthday to you!

JANELLE: Yes! Today is my birthday.

CHAPLAIN: O happy day!

JANELLE: I don't feel happy, Chaplain. I think I'm leading the rebellion in missing you.

CHAPLAIN: Now, don't you worry about a thing, Dear. I'm

alright and all like that.

JANELLE: You look like you're getting younger.

CHAPLAIN: I am.

JANELLE: Like your Horse Cavalry days. And you found Heaven?

CHAPLAIN: Heaven is found. It's all around, like Old Home Week.

JANELLE: Is it what you expected?

CHAPLAIN: Heaven is forever and it is right now.

JANELLE: What do you mean?

CHAPLAIN: Every day could be Heaven on Earth if you make it like it's someone's special birthday. Show up. Bring your gifts. Happy birthday, sweet Ji-neel.

JANELLE: But missing you makes it hard to celebrate.

CHAPLAIN: That's alright. All that is, is love, you see. Feel right by that.

JANELLE: If it hurts, why is it right?

CHAPLAIN: Because you remember.

JANELLE: Remember what?

CHAPLAIN: Why it is. For you. For me. For everybody. Why we can still talk and talk and talk, and all like that. See?

JANELLE: Teach me to see.

CHAPLAIN: When I am ready, I will get my new orders to continue God's work.

JANELLE: You work in Heaven?

CHAPLAIN: A Chaplain's work is never done.

JANELLE: What do you mean by saying, when you are ready?

CHAPLAIN: When I have completely rejuvenated, I'll be ready. They are helping me here with that transition.

JANELLE: Who?

CHAPLAIN: All of them.

JANELLE: You mean, your loved ones?

CHAPLAIN: I never meet a stranger.

JANELLE: What about Helen and...

CHAPLAIN: Oh, we've talked and shared with everybody here. Helen is fine. She's so sweet. And Eddie Wilson is here too.

JANELLE: Who is Eddie Wilson?

CHAPLAIN: He flew over England and got shot down during the war. 1944. He wants me to give you something.

JANELLE: I don't know an Eddie Wilson.

CHAPLAIN: Well, I think you do! And he sends this

message of love along for you to share with your English mate.

JANELLE: Eddie Wilson. Okay.

CHAPLAIN: Right, yeah, right. See, he's helping me prepare for the job of serving the soldiers who have died in Iraq.

JANELLE: Oh my goodness, Chaplain.

CHAPLAIN: That's right. And everything good is God with an extra O in it! And O, there is so much work to be done. Since your birthday back in 2003, nearly fifteen hundred and thirty-one of my men have died in this war for freedom.

JANELLE: And women.

CHAPLAIN: That's right, women too, and God does not differentiate or discriminate. No matter who we are, we all are welcome to receive all of God's love and help and guidance. I'm over here with a team of leaders to help deliver the message and to welcome and comfort each of these good men and women who have paid the supreme price for freedom, for all people all over the world, you see.

JANELLE: I think I'm getting the picture.

CHAPLAIN: Tell me what you see.

JANELLE: On Christmas morning, when I was still in mourning over you, I read your obituary in the paper. Your picture and story appeared just above a young Marine's who was only 21 when he was killed in Iraq.

CHAPLAIN: I've seen him.

JANELLE: You have?

CHAPLAIN: He is a fine young fellow. I'll be talking with him soon.

JANELLE: This is overwhelming for me.

CHAPLAIN: Now, with all this good news, why are you still crying?

JANELLE: I don't know. Maybe I'm being selfish. Maybe I'm afraid.

CHAPLAIN: What can I do to help you?

JANELLE: I guess I still have questions.

CHAPLAIN: Ask and you shall receive.

JANELLE: Since my dream the night you died, I have been terrified.

CHAPLAIN: Tell me all about it. I've got all the time in the world.

JANELLE: I was climbing up a slippery mountain slope looking for a hand or a rope to save me from falling. You were there at the top, holding on to a big white cross. So I kept climbing, trying to reach you, fighting against the forces of storm, wind and rain. You reached out your hand for me to take. I grabbed 'hold and when I finally reached the top, you smiled and nodded, *well done*.

CHAPLAIN: Go on.

JANELLE: Then you led me to the cross and placed my

palms upon its sturdy beam. There we stood together and we prayed. When the winds stopped whirring I awakened, struggling to remember what you said to me in the dream.

CHAPLAIN: What do you think I said?

JANELLE: Somehow in the blur of remembering, I am forgetting.

CHAPLAIN: Keep your eyes on the cross.

JANELLE: Is that what you said?

CHAPLAIN: Keep your eyes on the cross. In doing so you will remember where you came from, who sent you, and why you are here.

JANELLE: What do you mean?

CHAPLAIN: Keep it simple, Ji-neel, and get the job done.

JANELLE: Oh.

CHAPLAIN: O Ji-neel! My Ji-neel!

JANELLE: Thank you for coming back, Chaplain Barber.

CHAPLAIN: Thank you for remembering me.

JANELLE: I'll always remember this day, like it's our Memorial Day. Will we talk again?

CHAPLAIN: You will know the answer when we do.

JANELLE: It's time for you to go now, isn't it?

CHAPLAIN: It's time for you to heal and to feel good knowing there is so much we can do to help one another.

JANELLE: Goodbye for now, my Chaplain.

CHAPLAIN/JANELLE: And so it is.

Risen in my heart eternal like Jesus, my Chaplain is alive again. And so are all our loved ones and their loved ones too, when we choose to remember them, when we accept we're all on a mission from God. In this knowing, God is showing me His power, His presence, and there is peace, a new piece of the truth that has set me free.

* * *

ANNOUNCEMENTS

With loving thanks to all those who have been of service, immeasurable, throughout this experience. Simply said, we couldn't have done this without you.
Singing your praises, O!

Hymn #311 "*Thank You, Father*" ...Father in Heaven

Hymn #007 "*Onward Christian Soldier*" ...Grandpa in Heaven

Hymn #77 "*Best Friend-O-Topia*" ...Isabelle

Hymn #53 "*Dinner, Errands, Sitting, Rides*" ...Tata & Papa

Hymn #745 "*Unity, Editing, Talks*" ...Mom

Hymn #29 "*The Marine Corps Hymn*" ...Papa Hank

Hymn #805 "*Word of the Day, Prayers & Push*" ...Ellie

Hymn #12 "*Writers' Group Therapy*" ...Kelly & Class

Hymn #11 "*Presence, Peace & Power Puff*" ...Mikayla

Hymn #6 "*We're on a Mission From God*" ...Marlena

Hymn #1 "*Coffee-Tea-English-Wow!*" ...Kevin McSheffu

Hymn #21 "*Living History*" ...Hopefuls & pals at GWHS

Hymn #48 "*Woman's Best Friend*" ...Duke & Mario

Hymn #5 "*Builder is Best*" ...Les Demoiselles de Laguna

Special Thanks to the folks at the Riley Museum Home for James and all they do. Teresa at Mosaic Media Group/JALMA Music. Pam at Thurber House. Barbara & Nicole with good news. Jo Ellen Allen for her father's poem. Susan for her voice. *O Walt Whitman! To words in the American dream!* Barbara with Park Avenue Church history. Ed Royce for being one of the nation's best Congressmen, ever. Chris Hennen and Bob Searl for their thoughts, personally. Lynn Hernandez for "blowing my cover" with class. And heartfelt appreciation to the Barber Family for sharing their Papa with me.

STUDY GUIDE
ON-LINE REFERENCE
DIRECTORY

It's a certainty this list is limited. It could go on and on, like history. For now, please find this internet tour useful. These are the websites that directly link to some of the people, places and organizations that help explain Chaplain Barber's story so far and then some. Splendid surfing.

CHAPLAIN BARBER'S OFFICIAL SITE
www.livingdday.com

LINK TO THIS BOOK/PUBLISH YOURS
www.trafford.com

THE CHAPLAINCY
Army Chaplain Service
www.goarmy.com/chaplain

US Air Force Chaplain Service
www.usafhc.af.mil

National chaplain links
www.the911site.com

Chief of Chaplains
www.chapnet.army.mil

HISTORY/MUSEUMS

California Oral History Project
www.militarymuseum.org

National D-Day Museum
www.ddaymuseum.org

CHARITY/PHILANTHROPY

America's Promise
www.americaspromise.org

Operation Homefront
www.operationhomefront.net
1-800-779-5921

World Vision
www.wvi.org

Douglas M. Lawson (*Volunteering*)
www.douglawson.com

Samaritan's Purse
www.samaritanspurse.org

G.I.N.A./Jannel Rap
www.jannelrap.com
www.411gina.org

Angeles Crest Christian Camp
www.angelescrest.com

(Frank Kaleb Jansen) reference:
www.adoptapeople.org

Global Health Mission
www.ghm.org

PRACTICAL CHRISTIANITY

Help for Veterans and links
www.hhv.org

(Vets w/PTSD)
www.ncptsd.org/facts/veterans/fshelpforvets.html

Assist Ministries
www.assistnews.net

Ministries/Publications:
www.christianitytoday.com
www.guideposts.org
www.unityonline.org

Billy Graham:
www.billygraham.org
www.decisionmag.org

Focus on the Family
www.family.org
(International) www.ilsinternational.org

ORDER BIBLES

The Gideons International
www.gideons.org

COLLEGES/UNIVERSITIES
www.cincybible.org
www.hillsdale.edu/imprimus
www.harvard.edu
www.unl.edu

WORLD WAR II LINKS
http://www.fsu.edu/ww2/ www.military.com

STATESMANSHIP
www.statesman.org

Learn about your leaders:
www.house.gov/writerep

CHURCH REFERENCES

National Presbyterian Church:
www.natpresch.org

National Cathedral
www.cathedral.org

Disciples of Christ
www.disciples.org

Park Avenue Christian Church
www.parkavenuecc.com

Church of the Valley/Little Brown Church
www.covonline.org

MILITARY BASE/CB'S SERVICE SITES

Camp Lockett
www.militarymuseum.org/CpLockett.html

11th Horse Cavalry
www.geocities.com/fredlink/history.html www.geocities.
com/Pentagon/Barracks/2189/ www.horse101.com/topics/
History/cavalry_horse_html

Fort Benning
www.benning.army.mil

Camp Beale
www.beale.af.mil

Sierra Army Depot
www.sierra.army.mil

Fort Ord
http://nimst.tripod.com/cgi-bin/FtOrd.html

Camp Cooke
www.militarymuseum.org/CpCooke.html

Queen Mary
www.queenmary.com

AMERICAN CEMETERIES/MEMORIALS/TRIBUTE SITES

National D-Day Memorial (Bedford, VA.)
www.dday.org

American Battle Monuments Commission:
www.abmc.gov
www.arlingtoncemetery.net

Dwight D. Eisenhower:
www.presidentsusa.net/eisenhower.html

Omar N. Bradley:
www.arlingtoncemetery.net/omarnels.htm

George S. Patton: www.generalpatton.org
www.pattonhq.com
www.luxembourg.co.uk/nmmh/patton.html

AUTHOR'S INSPIRATIONS

Bob Searl's WWII Memories:
www.pbase.com/rhssr/after_dday

Daughters of the American Revolution:
www.dar.org

James Whitcomb Riley:
www.rileykids.org

Walt Whitman:
www.charityadvantage.com/waltwhitman

James Thurber:
www.thurberhouse.org

Ellie Michaels:
www.elliemichaelsmusic.com

30 Good Minutes:
www.30goodminutes.org

Southland Collie Rescue:
www.collie.org

"Hap" Arnold:
www.wasp-wwii.org/wasp/haparnold.htm

*William R. Arnold:
www.arlingtoncemetery.net/wrrichar.htm

*William Richard Arnold, The World War II Chief of Chaplains, was the first chaplain in United States military history to rise to the rank of General. He also penned a (missing) manuscript entitled "Soldiers of God" which is unrelated to any current publication of the same title.

During my visit with his memorial site I crossed my heart and tried not to cry. Then came the visions of my Chaplain standing in his office in Washington D.C. I cleared away tears from my burning eyes and prayed my sorrowful soul would not stay too long in the night my Grandfather died. I saved the Catholic priest to favorite memory and fled the scene searching for his soldiers of God. In faith I intend to locate his writings someday.

Joy and recovery can be found in history. I uncovered both in Chaplain Barber's rich story. Deep in labor-of-love study, steadily walking, talking and sharing with God, I'm toeing a most important line of love. Along your walk I wish you wings of the dove, fellowship, eternal friends, all of the above. Give voice to your discoveries. Share your good news with me. Let's work together to bring about hope in hearts, joy in preaching, blessings and the likeness of Jesus teaching, the Holy Spirit at work in all of us, *the truth that makes us free.* This could be, some may sing, the Red, White and Blue in you and me.

Janelle T. Frese: jtrising@aol.com

ABOUT THE AUTHOR

Janelle became a *Daughter of the American Revolution* upon her high school graduation in 1985. She earned a full ride to the University of Nebraska where she competed on the *Lady 'Huskers* NCAA Division I, three-time Big Eight and two-time Regional Championship softball team. She is a member of *Delta Delta Delta* national sorority and holds a masters degree in Instructional Leadership from National University.

She is a single mother and has been teaching full-time near her hometown of La Palma, California, for fifteen years. She currently serves students attending the local continuation high school where she is developing *The Hopefuls* project, alternative teens paired with special needs children, healing the heart of service through performance art. This program is designed to build a better community of understanding while restoring the human spirit.

Besides being a skilled artist and musician, Reiki master, certified massage technician and part-time commercial model and actress, Janelle is a versatile athlete having played professionally with *Ladies League Baseball*, 1997-1998. When she's not working, volunteering, tutoring, coaching or tinkering with her '63 Ford Falcon, every morning she writes.

"...*with God all things are possible.*" (Matthew 19:26)

ISBN 1-41204354-9